"JEREMY TURNER takes the readers on a ride of pain, reality, love, and answering God's call—all within a quick read! This is a must-read for those who want to see how one truly lives out their calling to protect and to serve."

—MATT SLAPPEY

"MOST OF US have had trying times to get through. After a series of shocking events, Jeremy Turner shares his extraordinary journey moving through his grief and transforming his life into one that is inspiring. He challenges us all to look at ourselves and ask, 'How are we doing?' It is a real-life example of the mustard seed: in serving others, we heal ourselves."

—MARTHA DEMERE

TO PROTECT AND SERVE

HOW ONE OFFICER SOUGHT TO CHANGE THE WORLD

JEREMY TURNER

Edited by Blake Atwood of BA Writing Solutions LLC: blakeatwood.com

Cover design by Erin New

To learn more or to donate to Contribute2America, visit Contribute2America.org.

To contact Jeremy Turner, email jeremy.turner@contribute2america.org or call 404-406-4088.

For my brother, John,

and all the families and homeless people

who have inspired me to do what I do

PROLOGUE

GOD HAS A PLAN.

I've always believed that.

Through losing those close to me, enduring a divorce, and having been a police officer who's witnessed the worst the world can do to a person, I *still* believe God has a plan—for me *and* for you.

What you're about to read is my story of how an imperfect man became a police officer and then launched his own nonprofit, Contribute2America. Ultimately, this is my history of hope despite loss, love despite evil, and healing despite adversity.

Certainly, I want you to learn more about our nonprofit, but it's my sincere hope and prayer that, as you read my story, you'll find yourself somewhere within its pages. Whether that means you're the person who needs help or you're the person who needs to be a helper is for you to decide.

Either way, God has a plan for you.

You'll soon see that I've always believed that.

PART 1

JOHN

CHAPTER 1

YOU'RE JOKING

IN 1998, on a sweltering July day in Atlanta, I drove home from work with hundred-degree air blasting me in the face. My air conditioning had been shot for months. Consequently, every time I shifted my weight, the back of my button-up shirt would peel itself off the hot leather seat. I'd resettle myself, feel that temporary reprieve of coolness from my own sweat, then complain internally about my piece-of-junk car.

The hot air was stifling, so I loosened my tie to breathe better.

It's a good thing I did.

As soon as I'd untied that professional noose, my phone rang. "Hello?" I didn't hear anything for a second—just a deep inhalation.

"Jeremy, it's . . . it's Jared."

I knew immediately that something was wrong. My younger brother's tone was off, and he'd stumbled over his words in less than a second. "What's wro—"

He cut me off before I could get the words out. "It's about Jonathan."

"What's *wrong*, Jared?"

"He's been in an accident. He's been killed."

My already-flushed face grew redder. "This isn't funny, moron."

Jared paused. "I'm not joking, brother."

Silence.

My brother spoke next. "He's really gone, Jeremy. I'm sorry."

In a brief moment of clarity, I reasoned with myself: *His tone hasn't changed. He wouldn't take such a sick joke this far. Which means he's telling the truth.*

With the world still speeding by and my internal world going upside down, I pulled over.

On the side of road on July 17, during a sweltering summer day in Atlanta, I listened to my younger brother tell me how our older brother, John, had died that day.

CHAPTER 2

STILL ALIVE

JOHN WASN'T JUST the older brother I needed. He was the one I would have chosen had I been given the choice.

I needed him because I'd been a premie. For most of my young life and on into my adolescence, I suffered from ear problems, nasal problems, stomach problems, and developmental issues. But God must have known what he was doing by ensuring that John was my older brother. In those years when I felt so weak, John was my guardian angel—the big brother who protected me, challenged me, encouraged me, and inspired me.

I also needed him because we were children of divorce. When I was three, which would have made John five years old and my sister six, our parents split. Like so many other kids of my generation, we lived with our mom and visited our dad every other weekend. Amid the chaos of a broken home, John was my constant.

Gratefully, my parents didn't have a bitter separation, but there were hardships. For example, our father stopped financially providing for us, which meant our mother had to pick up extra shifts in her nursing career. She even took on another job during the holidays at a local toy store so that we'd still be able to have a wonderful Christmas—which we did.

Because money was tight, we seldom if ever received new things. Most of our clothes were hand-me-downs. Our food was purchased in bulk. Our list of chores was long, and it had to be completed before Mom got home from her shift. Somehow—likely under John's leadership—it always got done. Looking back, it's rather obvious: John had to step in and be our father figure in some respects.

I needed John for his strength and protection when I was young. I also needed him to be the role model I'd lost in my dad. But I would have *chosen* John to be my older brother because of his character. He was the kind of man everyone seemed to look up to. He was smart, handsome, *and* a great athlete. And he always seemed to handle life's circumstances calmly and with a smile.

Of course, I wanted to be like my big brother when I grew up.

But, once we had grown up, he took a different professional path than the one I chose.

During his sophomore year at the University of Georgia, John enlisted in the Marines. We hailed from a military family; my mother had met my father when he was in the Air Force. Plus, in 1990, no one could escape the constant barrage of news about conflicts in the Middle East. He was compelled to serve his country and do his duty for others —for us.

As he liked to say, "First to go, last to know." For too long, I didn't know what he meant, but, in hindsight, I understand. During his deployment, it seemed like the Marines were always the first ones sent into combat when something terrible was taking place. It was probably better for my nerves during his combat time that I didn't know how dangerous his days actually were.

John's tour of duty took him to the Middle East, Guantanamo Bay, and Haiti. We wouldn't hear from him for months. Of course, our family worried about him every day. I often wondered what he was doing. I'd imagine him playing football on his downtime, giving toys or candy to children while on duty and providing cover fire for his fellow soldiers on whatever raid they might have had that day.

But then I'd get a letter with his name at the top left corner of the envelope. I'd tear it open as soon as it reached my hands. I'd scan it quickly, then I'd reread it slowly. He couldn't tell me where he was or what he was doing, but he always wrote positively about his mission.

As I read, I'd flash back to our adventures together: when he taught me to shoot my first rifle; when he taught me to drive a stick shift; when we bought our first car together. Or the all-too-memorable day when I wrecked my bike and he carried me home. These letters and flashbacks would often make me cry. Over and over, I'd realize: *John's always been there for me.* Then I'd pray, *Please, God, let him come home. When's he's done serving, I need him to always be* here *for me.*

I loved those letters, but not necessarily because of what he told me through his words. Getting the letter itself represented something better: my brother was still alive.

CHAPTER 3

SOWING SEEDS

WHEN I'D READ my brother's letters, I'd hear his voice in my head as if he were right next to me speaking what he'd written. I couldn't help but think, *How did John become John? How did my brother become such an excellent man of character?*

Then an indelible image would spring to mind: the North Georgia mountains—specifically, the mountains just behind our grandparents' place.

My grandparents, Hubert and Lucille Turner, were blue-collar workers raised during the Great Depression. They knew what it meant to *work*. My grandmother was a librarian at the county's high school. My grandfather drove a logging truck. Their lives revealed that they practiced what they preached: you have to work and save for every dollar you earn.

So, of course, they taught us the true definition of work.

While my grandfather still had to drive his truck during the summers we stayed with them, my grandmother busied herself with their family garden. Today, when I think of her,

I see her two- to three-acre garden filled with produce ranging from corn, okra, and tomatoes to potatoes and green beans.

Most of those golden-memory mornings had the same routine: We'd wake to the smell of a fantastically prepared breakfast of homemade biscuits, country ham, and fresh eggs. (What I wouldn't give for that breakfast today.) Hymns like "Amazing Grace" would be gently wafting through the air, a constant backing soundtrack to these fond memories. After devouring our meal, my grandmother would head out of her front door, holding it open until we'd passed through, then join us in the garden.

Then it was a few hours of *hard* work. We'd pick weeds, pull produce, shuck corn, peel potatoes, and harvest green beans. If we finished the outside work, my grandmother always had something more for us to do. For instance, she was always preparing for the winter, so we'd help her can produce and make soup, applesauce, and prepared meals.

My grandmother also made sure we knew our Bibles. At night, even despite my weariness, I would jump into my grandmother's bed as she read her Bible aloud. She'd let me read a few verses, and then she'd explain to me what I'd just read. She had a knack for clarifying and simplifying the Bible so I could both understand it and apply it to my life. (Even as I became an adult, I would still call her when something in the Bible didn't add up to me!)

Through her patience with me as a child, I learned how we ought to treat people and to help those who can't help themselves. Looking back from decades later, it amazes me how God has used those specific, simple lessons in mighty ways in my life—as if my grandmother wasn't just a sower of seeds in her garden.

But we'll get to that.

No doubt: those summers were tough on us as kids, but they were the anvil against which our character was forged.

CHAPTER 4

FIELD BROTHERS

UNFORTUNATELY, every summer ends.

But, for John and me, the close of summer meant the beginning of something much more important to both of us.

Football.

We lived in Norcross, Georgia, which is about fifteen minutes northeast of Atlanta. And for just about anywhere in the South, football is *big*.

Throughout elementary, John and I often played on the same football team. To make it easier on my mom, I had moved up from playing on a team with my friends to playing on John's team. Prior to that, my single mom had had to drive to multiple locations for practices and games. Eventually, practicality won out. But that meant I was playing with kids two years older—and I was already short for my age.

Even though I was smaller than most everyone on the field, I made up for my size disadvantage by being faster and hitting harder. It didn't hurt that I knew my brother had my back, that he was always watching over me, cheering me on, and inspiring me to keep playing as hard as I could. Of course, I wanted to impress him too.

John was a fantastic athlete—big and strong and well-suited for football. We played on the same team right up until John started middle school and was eligible for the school team. I was sad for us to be separated in that way, but I was also happy that I'd get to play football with my friends again.

In 1986, John transferred to Admiral Farragut Academy in St. Petersburg, Florida. He continued to excel in football and was voted All-Conference for both offense and defense in both his junior and senior years. He even received that prestigious award from Heisman Trophy winner Vinny Testaverde.

Ever the follow-after younger brother, I asked our mom if I could also attend Admiral Farragut. To my surprise, particularly concerning the additional expense of sending me to this private school, my mother said yes. I don't know how she made it happen, but she knew how important it was to me to be close to John. She'd probably known about our inseparable bond since my birth.

I joined John at Admiral Farragut Academy during my sophomore year, which was his senior year. I made the Varsity team and played football alongside my brother once again. As a star player on a small squad, John seldom left the field. He was a phenom on both offense and defense, though he typically played linebacker or running back while I played strong safety. We were the Turner brothers looking after each other on the field yet again.

Gratefully, my brother hadn't turned into a Big Man on Campus with no time for his little brother outside of football. Because we were from Atlanta, we stayed on campus. (Most students went home on the weekends or for holidays.)

And because no student cars were allowed at our school, we rode our bikes to nearby beaches, sometimes as far as twenty miles away.

We also made fast friends with other students who shared our predicament of being far from home. For instance, Nevil Cork was a fellow student from Hilton Head, South Carolina. While we liked Nevil, we may have liked his connections more. He knew a guy who lived right across from the school and who owned a motorcycle. What made this beneficial to John and me was that this generous fellow allowed us to borrow his motorcycle, which opened up a world of possibilities to us during our downtime at the Admiral.

For a little while, this motorcycle gave us access to the other beautiful beaches and marshes in Florida, where we'd fish. We'd never done any saltwater fishing before; I fell in love with it. When we had spent time in the north Georgia Mountains, John and I liked to fish, mostly catching rainbow and brown trout in the local mountain streams. Being from North Georgia and being an avid fly fisherman, catching redfish and sea trout opened my eyes to a new style of fishing those beautiful coastal waters in Florida. The motorcycle helped because we could find new fishing holes. John was better at driving the motorcycle than me, so, for every place we adventured to, I just drew it all in.

What I'm trying to say is that John and I did just about everything together. And we never got bored because we were always with each other.

After graduating, John could have played football at any number of smaller colleges, but something even more important than football was swaying his decision. In the summer of 1987, John declared that he would attend the

University of Georgia—because his girlfriend was already a Bulldog.

Two years into his time at UGA, John felt the tug that all enlisted service members must feel: *I can do something more with my life.* He quit school and joined the Marines, as you've already read. He'd leave us for months at a time, resulting in those letters that made me cry.

Then his tour of duty was over, and John returned to the safe shores of these United States. He went back to college free of charge thanks to the GI Bill and earned a degree in AutoCAD Engineering.

Which is why listening to my younger brother describe John's death was all the more confusing.

He could have died in the many war zones he'd been in, but he wasn't supposed to die *after* his deployment.

How could this have happened?

CHAPTER 5

WHAT HAPPENED

I SAT in my car in a trance-like state as my younger brother told me how our older brother had been killed earlier that day.

"Coming home from work, driving down I-985 just like any other day, John saw a stranded woman on the side of the road. She was trying to change her flat tire, and John saw she had a small baby with her as well. So, of course, John stopped to help."

Even though we were on the phone, I nodded my head.

Jared continued. "The woman was thrilled that he'd stopped. She told him that so many people had passed her by already. That she felt helpless. And that the immense heat wasn't helping. John reassured her that everything would be OK, that he'd get her tire back on, and she'd be back on the road in no time."

I nodded again. I may have even smiled, thinking about how my brother John was always a helper. But that smile quickly faded with the understanding of where this story was inevitably headed.

"John got the jack and the tire-changing tools out of the woman's car, went to the busted tire, his back to the highway, and started the process of changing the tire. Minutes later, with John still on one knee by the tire, a speeding white van struck and killed him."

I started crying.

"I was told—and this is hard to hear, brother—that his body was sent flying more than twenty feet away. The van stopped about a hundred yards after impact. John laid lifeless in the middle of the highway until police and fire rescue arrived on the scene. They pronounced him dead at the scene of the accident."

A thousand thoughts coursed through my shattered mind as my brother told me a story I didn't want to believe was true.

It wasn't enemy gunfire or an RPG attack he'd become accustomed to during his tour in the Gulf War that had killed him. He hadn't died in one of the deadliest places on earth at the time. Rather, as we would come to learn, he was struck and killed on the side of the road by a man driving a white van while high on cocaine and methamphetamines.

To make matters even more maddening and confusing, we also later learned that *multiple* calls to 911 had been made prior to the accident. Many people had witnessed the erratic white van swerving down the highway, nearly hitting several cars along the way. But the police couldn't get to him —at least, not until his van had stopped about a hundred yards after striking and killing my older brother.

To be honest, I don't really recall what my brother Jared said to me on the phone that day. I know he told me about what happened, but, in the shock of the moment, all I heard was the mumble of his voice while flashbacks of my time with my brother played themselves on a loop within the theater of my mind.

I didn't want to admit to myself what had happened.

John was gone.

CHAPTER 6

GOOD SAMARITAN

ONE PART of the story that didn't shock me was that John died as a Good Samaritan. But even that part of the story has more to tell.

A few days after John's death, I spoke with the woman he'd helped. I thought it might help ease my pain to talk with her since she'd been the last one to see him alive.

When I finally contacted her, I could tell that she was still upset by the incident. We both were, so it was an awkward conversation at first.

I corroborated the police report with what she had witnessed. Nothing she told me veered from what had been reported. But, right before our conversation was going to end, she said, "Your brother saved me and my baby's lives."

Not knowing what to say, I simply replied, "I know." I thought she was referring to the fact that, if he hadn't stopped to help, they could have gotten hit or something else bad could have happened to a stranded woman and her small child.

Then, as if she'd heard my thoughts, she replied, "No, it's not just that he stopped to help us. A few seconds before he was hit, I was standing next to him, and I was holding my baby. I was watching him change my tire and thanking him for stopping. He looked up at me with a smile and kindly asked me to go stand on the other side of the vehicle because it wasn't safe for me to stand next to him. I'd barely walked around the car, by the middle of the hood, and that's when—"

She couldn't finish her sentence, but she didn't need to.

I replied, "Thank you for telling me that."

At that moment, I wondered if God had been speaking through my brother or if John's keen sense for others' safety had kicked in, resulting in his warning the woman to get on the other side of the car. Had he not encouraged her to move, there very likely could have been three dead people on the side of the road that day.

But there was only one.

After Jared had told me about how John had died, and after I'd composed myself at least enough to drive, I went to the hospital where they'd taken John's body.

Upon arrival, I learned that my mom had passed out. Once she'd come to, she'd taken a sedative to calm her down. John's wife couldn't stop crying. It felt like a war zone where all my family members were the walking wounded. Or it was a nightmare from which I'd never awake. And because I was closest to John, everyone was looking to me for answers—which I didn't have.

The hospital staff had placed my brother's body in a small family room. They asked if I wanted to see him. I did, of course, but I was tentative upon my approach. I didn't know what to expect. Before opening the door to the room in which he lay, I stepped back. I took a deep breath. And then I entered.

My older brother, the man whom I most admired and

always wanted to be like, laid cold, lifeless, and blood-stained on a dull metal table. His clothes had been ripped to shreds. I should have expected as much, but I was still shocked to see him like that.

Still, I walked over to him, placed my head on his chest, and sobbed.

I held his cold hand and thought, *Why him, God? Why him?*

I don't know how long I stayed there like that. I didn't want to say good-bye.

Eventually, I let go of his hand, but I would never let go of his memory.

CHAPTER 7

IF ONLY

DEATH ALWAYS HAS a way of putting life into perspective.

On the long drive home from the hospital that night, all I wanted to do was to hug my wife and daughter.

To be honest, our marriage was struggling at this point—something I'll share more about in a later chapter—but for that night, we put our differences aside and prayed for my brother's wife and my extended family.

Following that, I rocked Hannah, our one-and-a-half-year-old delight of a baby girl, a little longer than usual. As I got lost in gazing at her face, I wondered how I'd feel if I ever lost her. I thought about what my mom and dad must have been experiencing that night. No parent should lose their child, regardless of how old that child is.

I thought about how devastating it was to lose my brother—but to lose your daughter? Your son? It was so unimaginably horrific to me that my mind—or my deep grief—prevented me from considering it. I prayed for my parents and our family, asking God to give us strength for the days ahead and to watch over our grieving family.

After putting Hannah to bed, my mind was racing. I couldn't sleep—not after the day I'd had. I walked into my office and stared out of the window.

This is all just a bad dream. It has to be. In just a minute, I'm going to wake up as if nothing's happened. John will call me and I'll hear his voice one more time, and I'll tell him how much he's always meant to me. If only I could wake up from this nightmare.

I never went to sleep that night, which meant my nightmare was real. There would be no call. Life would go on, whether I felt like it should or not.

Bright light pierced my face as the sun rose on the day after my brother's death. At that moment, God met me. I heard him speak these simple, comforting words to my soul: "Everything's going to be OK, Jeremy."

I breathed a momentary sigh of relief. I believed those words. In the coming days and months, I would cling to them.

My first uphill battle was a family fight over what no family wants to fight about: my brother's funeral arrangements. John's wife wanted him to be cremated. My family wanted John to have a military burial, which meant having a more traditional service where the body would not be cremated.

I somehow became the arbiter for this argument.

Unfortunately, my brother and I had never discussed his funeral arrangements. I didn't know if he'd want to be cremated or buried. What brothers in their twenties, who believe they'll live many years longer, talk about these things?

But a decision had to be made and made quickly. Tensions rose, complicated all the more by the shock and devastation of losing our beloved John. All I wanted to do was run away and grieve on my own. But when I had those rather selfish thoughts, I asked myself a question I'd often asked myself before: *What would John do?*

John would find a way to build a bridge between warring parties.

In the end, John was cremated *and* we had a military funeral that honored his sacrificial service to his country.

Though we laid him to rest two weeks later, John's wife, April, was still my friend, and I know she loved my brother more than anything. I wanted to do what I could to help her because I knew she was struggling. Later that year, April and I took John's ashes up to the top of Mount Yonah, where John I had grown up hiking and camping. We threw some of his ashes off of the mountain, a symbolic moment for me, as it was for her. I'd like to thank her for letting me be a part of that experience.

I still think about John every day. I've thought, *If only the police could have caught that driver sooner. If only John hadn't been such a nice guy. If only I could have had more time with him.*

And I've thought, *If only he were still here, would he be proud of me?*

PART 2

ROBERT

CHAPTER 8

YET AGAIN

FOUR MONTHS after my brother's death, I received yet another phone call that would forever alter my life.

On that cool November day, I was sitting at my sales desk at work when my phone rang. As a salesman, I picked up quickly. You never knew when the next sale might just call you instead of you having to call them.

"Jeremy?"

My sister, Stephanie, sounded strange. That same sense I'd had when Jared had called me about John invaded my soul. Something sounded very off. "What's wrong?"

"It's Dad. He was shot and killed during a robbery."

"What do you mean?"

I'd heard what she said, but the shock was too much. I had to hear her say it again for her words to actually make sense.

She repeated herself, then she told me the unfortunate, tragic details.

Again, just as in my conversation with my brother only a few months back, I mostly heard mumbles. She spoke clearly enough, but the thoughts racing through my mind muddled her voice. Even as she shared the details of his killing, all I heard within was, *How could this have happened—again?*

As for what actually happened, some context is in order.

CHAPTER 9

HIS LIFE

WHEN I WAS BORN, my parents lived in Atlanta. My dad was a lineman for Georgia Power, which meant he did the grunt work of actually fixing and maintaining power lines throughout the county. I was often told war stories about bad storms and late nights spent repairing downed power lines.

My mother was a nurse. They both worked long hours and odd shifts. In time, these scheduling rifts opened chasms in their relationship that would never be bridged. They divorced when I was three.

You know some of this already.

What you may not know is that both of our parents still loved us. Some children from broken homes have fathers who, once cut free from their spouse, cut themselves free from their family responsibilities. That wasn't my father.

Even though he couldn't help support us financially in the years after the divorce, we were still the recipients of his love. We spent many weekends camping and picnicking on top of Mount Yonah in Cleveland, Georgia. And I fondly remember when my dad would take John, my sister, and me to Lake Lanier Islands, a resort complex, to see Jimmy Buffett (a tradition I still follow with my children when Buffett comes to Atlanta). As my father grew older and his career trajectory went upward, he began contributing financially to our well-being.

Looking back on my childhood, I cherished those every-other-weekend visits.

When my sister told me my father had been killed, *his* life—at least what I knew of it—flashed before my eyes.

I saw the North Georgia mountains behind my grandparents' place, the same mountains that had shadowed my dad while he was growing up.

I caught a glimpse of my dad throwing down his last hay bale, a determined look on his face, knowing that he'd be leaving farm work behind after eighteen years of seeming non-stop work.

I watched as he earned his wings when joining the Air Force.

I smiled as he met my mom while he was stationed in Missouri and she was still in college.

I heard their wedding bells toll as they married just a few months later.

I felt their beaming pride as Stephanie was born at the Whiteman Air Force Base.

I watched over their shoulders as the last remaining soldiers in Vietnam were helicoptered out on TV.

I rode with them and all their worldly possessions back to Cleveland, Georgia, where they'd stay with my grandmother until they could find a job.

Then I rode back with them to Norcross, Georgia, and saw how ecstatic they were to welcome John, and then me, into their world.

And then I heard my dad's voice—a voice I suddenly realized I'd never hear again—regaling me with more stories about his life.

"Jeremy, back when you were little, I worked my lineman job *and* I attended law school. But I had to go to the law library at Emory because my law school at John Marshall didn't even have one!"

I think he liked to boast about how hard a worker he was. Or he was trying to teach me some lesson. Or he was just telling me the lengths he had to go to in order to succeed at his dreams.

Whatever his reason, I was impressed—especially to think that *my dad* could be a lawyer.

But, for reasons I'll never know, he graduated from John Marshall Law School but never practiced law.

Two years after the divorce, he remarried and entered the poultry sales force in Gainesville, Georgia, a job he would stay at for years. My stepmother, Frances, was great, and she loved all of us as her own children. Thank you, Frances, for your support and for loving us.

During this time, he also became more involved in his church, Free Chapel. He was a devoted Christian who got involved in mission work. On multiple church-sponsored mission trips to Peru, he helped build several churches, assisted in establishing wells for fresh drinking water, and worked on a medical ship that traveled up and down the Amazon River.

I hadn't known this side of my dad when I was younger, but it was thrilling for me to see the light in his eyes when he spoke about these trips. I still distinctly remember the one time he'd returned from one of these trips and told me, "I feel like I have a calling to help people, but not in Peru. I want to help the down-and-out in Atlanta."

When he said that, I was proud of my father. But had I known that his calling would ultimately result in his death, I would have cautioned him against it.

But none of us can know the future, and we all have to follow God's calling on our lives—no matter where it leads.

CHAPTER 10

HIS CALLING

A YEAR before my brother John was killed, my father had launched Mission America, a nonprofit that sought to help inner-city families through a faith-based approach. This involved counseling and assistance with food and housing. My father also had plans to set up a mobile trailer that could go where needed so the gospel could be preached and sang about throughout the inner city.

Mission America's work—which was really just my father at the beginning—started in the West End of Atlanta, an area where my father believed a number of problems existed that he could help. In addition to launching several programs to help families with food and housing, he also purchased several homes to fix up for needy families. He even did much of the restoration and maintenance work on these homes to keep the budget down.

My father was killed while working on one of these houses.

When I hung up the phone after speaking with my sister on that fateful day, I wondered yet again, *Is this just another bad dream? When am I going to wake up from it? Why does this keep happening to our family?*

I thought about a news report I'd seen just the day before, about the murder rate in Atlanta. The report featured interviews with some of the victims' family members. Yesterday, those family members' words were just background news to my everyday life. They didn't seem real because they were on TV. But, on that day, with what I'd just heard from my sister, I realized, *I am them. And the pain and loss they feel are as real as anything.*

Later that evening, my family and I met at my father's house with his pastor. We all wanted answers to our one pressing question: Why?

The police hadn't given us much information since the investigation was still ongoing. But one of my father's employees at Mission America had witnessed the incident.

Apparently, my father needed a few nails, so he'd walked from the house on Cleveland Avenue to his truck. That's when he was confronted by a young black man with a gun. In just a few seconds, my dad got into a fight with his would-be killer. I don't know if my dad thought he could take the young-looking kid and wrestle the gun away from him or if my dad, who was always a hard worker, just didn't want to be robbed that day.

Whatever the reason, my father was shot as a result.

My father's employee had run outside as soon as he'd heard the fight, only to see the suspect shoot my father—twice. Then the young man stole my father's rings and his watch before running away.

In a tragic echo of what our family had only recently endured, we went through the laborious process of another police investigation into the senseless murder of a family member. For what it's worth, we were pleased with the cooperation we experienced from the City of Atlanta Police Investigators and the district attorney's office. It didn't take them long to catch the culprit who'd killed my father.

That young man is currently serving consecutive life sentences.

But what I wouldn't give for that man to be free and my father to still be alive.

PART 3

NICOL

CHAPTER 11

DEATH IN THREES

AFTER MY BROTHER *and* my father had been killed, I waited in quiet fear of what tragedy would happen next. Like popular opinion says, bad things happen in threes, right?

No one else in my family would come to their untimely end soon after my father's death, but something else died that had been withering for months.

Just after Christmas—just one month after we'd laid my father to rest—my wife told me she wanted a divorce.

I tried to reason with her, but she'd made up her mind. I asked if we could see a counselor, but she declined. She just wanted out.

I didn't fight her on it. I knew our marriage had been on its last legs for some time.

Ironically enough, I'd met my wife partially because of her legs. When I attended the University of Georgia, she was a cross country runner at Georgia State University. We had met while I was working at a local sporting goods store. We fell for each other quickly and chose to get married at a young age. Four years later, we welcomed our daughter, Hannah, into our family.

I thank God for Hannah, for so many reasons. As our divorce proceeded, Hannah was my lifeline, holding me together each day. All I knew was that I wanted to be the best dad for my then almost-two-year-old.

My wife and I chose an amicable divorce and we split all of our assets down the middle. We also sought joint custody of our daughter. My wife then moved into an apartment while I stayed in the house until it was sold.

Once the house sold, Hannah and I moved into an apartment in downtown Atlanta. She'd stay with me for four days during the week, and then she'd stay with her mother for three days.

During my time without Hannah, I worked fifteen-hour days so I could have more time off for the days when I had Hannah. I tried to do as much as possible with her on our days: football games, camping, hiking, going to the beach, sailing, and hanging out in the park.

When all I wanted to do was fall apart after having lost my brother, my father, and my marriage, Hannah kept me together.

The following year, nothing tragic occurred. As I grieved my marriage and the possible effects of divorce on our daughter, I also began to heal. I believe that God has a plan for everyone. Despite what had happened to me and my family, I knew God wanted to help us heal.

He first did that at my high school reunion, of all places.

I attended my 1999 reunion with my near-lifelong friend, Shane, who had also been recently divorced at the time. I believe it was helpful and healing for both Shane and me to commiserate about our failed marriages.

I also reconnected with my friend Sara, who'd lived in the house behind mine when we were children. Her family had moved from Vietnam into our neighborhood, and I'd been friends with her older brother.

At the time, Sara was in a serious relationship, so I knew there were boundaries to our relationship. But, after that reunion, we grabbed a few lunches and dinners together as friends. We spoke openly about life and relationships and what had happened to us in the many years since we'd last connected.

Just being with Sara, even as platonic as it was, gave me the confidence to get back into the dating scene.

And Sara, if you're reading this: Thank you. Thank you for the help and for instilling confidence in me to come out of a bad situation. Thank you for making me feel worthy when I felt worthless.

To Shane and my lifelong friends Joe and Chris: Thank you too. Through all of the tragedies I endured, I remain grateful for each one of you who were there for me. I could not have gotten through those years without you. I am truly blessed to say that I have friends, my personal band of brothers and sisters, who have encouraged, challenged, and loved me for decades.

Without you all, I never would have become emotionally healthy enough for the beginning of one of the best chapters of my life.

CHAPTER 12

LIFE REBOOTED

AT FIRST, following the divorce, my time with Hannah was scarce. I was working too many hours on a grueling schedule. But all I wanted to do was spend time with my daughter. So, in an effort to lessen my working burden during the days she was with me, I quit my job and purchased a pizzeria in Virginia Highlands, a trendy neighborhood close to where we lived. Chris, a friend of mine, managed the place.

Whenever Hannah was with her mother, I worked long, hard hours at the restaurant. This afforded me the opportunity to take off all the days Hannah was with me. I was grateful for those moments and that time with her.

On the days I worked, I'd often meet up after work with my friends Neil and Gary, who were Atlanta police officers, at our favorite dive, Taco Mac. That's where my life—outside of my times with Hannah—got happier.

Because, of course, I met a girl.

Nicol was a waitress and bartender at Taco Mac, and she caught my eye the first time I saw her. She was (and is) so beautiful.

She knew most of the officers who would routinely show up. I wondered if she'd ever gone out with any of them, but then one of my police buddies introduced me to her. Maybe he thought I'd had such a rough time that I needed to meet someone like Nicol.

He was right.

Over the next several weeks, we made small talk during my visits to her restaurant. She told me that she worked nights while attending nursing school during the day. Almost instantly, we had a point of connection. I couldn't help but think about how my mom's caring attitude had resulted in her nursing career too.

From our discussions and just the way she carried herself, I could tell she was an independent woman and could take care of herself with no problems. She was a bartender, after all, and I'm sure she'd had to deal with more than her fair share of over-zealous drunks. Her strong will attracted me.

Eventually, after a few months of these otherwise innocent talks, I mustered up the courage to ask her out.

She agreed, but I could tell she was hesitant. Not one to shy away from confrontation myself, I asked why.

She gave me an honest answer—yet another reason I wanted to date her. "I've never dated someone with a child. And, well, I'm recently divorced too. I kind of just want to be free for a while."

I nodded my head in agreement. Then I smiled. "I understand." But I wouldn't relent. "Why don't we talk about all of that over dinner?"

She laughed. "OK. You win."

We set a night for a date, but there was one problem, at least insofar as first dates go. My daughter would have to join us.

Since Nicol was in the restaurant business, she could only go to dinner during the week, and the date we set was a day when Hannah would be with me. At first, I didn't think it'd be a good idea to have such a strange first date. But, before the day arrived, I rethought my position. I reasoned with myself, *I don't have time to play games. I want Nicol to like me for who I am and the child I love and adore. We're a package deal.*

I took Nicol and Hannah to a new restaurant in Atlanta. While Nicol and I ate, my restless Hannah ran around the restaurant, hid under the tables, and sometimes pulled on our legs. In other words, she was a three-year-old.

But Nicol took it all in stride. She knew how to have a good time. In fact, Nicol seemed to really like Hannah, and I think Hannah liked Nicol too. I had the first inklings that this date could turn into something more.

We dated for several months. We danced together, exercised together, attended parties together, and watched football together. (I learned to accept that her favorite collegiate team was Alabama.) Nicol treated me with respect and loved me at a time when I felt less than lovable. It felt good to have that kind of companionship back in my life. And it was made all the better by Nicol's growing relationship with my daughter.

After several months of dating, Nicol took the initiative and asked Hannah and me to move in with her. Her condo was definitely better than our apartment, so we readily accepted. Her place even had an extra room that Hannah could have all to her own when she stayed with us.

I knew what my next step was, even though I think we were both nervous to walk down another aisle.

Nicol and I had been working hard for months, so I offered to take her on a long weekend getaway to a Florida coast bed and breakfast on Amelia Island called the Fairbanks House. We woke early for excellent breakfasts, strolled up and down the beach, ate superb dinners, and thoroughly enjoyed ourselves.

With each day there, I kept realizing just how amazing she was. I knew that I wanted to spend the rest of my life with her. So, after returning from the beach one day, I proposed to her—in the shower.

I couldn't even get down on one knee because the shower was so small.

And I didn't even have a ring—at least a real engagement ring. Instead, I presented her with a ring I'd purchased from a gas station bubblegum machine on our drive to the bed and breakfast. I told her it was just a placeholder until we returned to Atlanta and we could pick out her ring together.

Oh, and she said yes.

Six months later, Nicol and I returned to Amelia Island and were wed on the beach. We even stayed in the same room in which we'd gotten engaged. Since then, we've done our best to visit Fairbanks House for our anniversaries.

Shortly after the wedding, Nicol graduated from Georgia Baptist College with a bachelor of science in nursing and quickly landed a job. We were ready to move out of our condo, and we found a house not too far from where we'd been living.

Nicol became a great mother to Hannah, but Nicol also desired to have a child of her own. Nine months later, we welcomed Mary Grace, our little redhead, into our family.

When Nicol saw Mary's hair, she cried. "Where did that red hair come from?" She was shocked to see our little girl with such deeply red hair. Neither of us was a redhead —but both of our family lines had redheads. I assured Nicol that Mary Grace was, in fact, our baby.

As our small family of four was just getting its legs, the events of September 11, 2001, changed the world. Income from my business declined, possibly because consumers were becoming more conscious about their spending habits in the wake of the terrorist attacks. We started falling behind on bills, which always seems to be a precursor to relationship trouble.

I sat down with Nicol and told her I'd start looking for another job—something stable and, most importantly at that time, with benefits that would cover our family.

If there was one thing I'd learned from both my brother and my father, a man takes care of his family.

I knew I had to step up if I didn't want this marriage to end like my last one.

Plus, I wanted my job to have meaning.

I wanted to make a difference.

PART 4

OFFICER TURNER

CHAPTER 13

TIRE HELL

BECAUSE OF WHAT our family had endured during the murders and subsequent investigations into my brother and my father's deaths, I chose to become a police officer.

I'd witnessed firsthand how the officers had helped our family find resolution during a traumatic time. I saw that what they were doing really affected people's lives for the better.

For as much flak as officers receive for when things go wrong, then and even now, they seem to receive far less notice for when things go right, or even better than right. And now that I've been an officer for seventeen years, I can tell you: we strive our best to get things right.

In 2001, I applied to the two largest police agencies in the state: the City of Atlanta and DeKalb County. The agencies split coverage of the Atlanta area. Crime was rampant throughout. No matter where I ended up, I was sure to be worked hard.

The hiring process was thorough. This included multiple written exams and a physical training test. The DeKalb County police department offered me a position first, which I gladly accepted. They were well-known throughout the country for their training—and I sure did get trained.

The DeKalb training was six months of an arduous new officer boot camp. Honestly, it was hell.

In fact, it was hell with a tire.

After our first week, each recruit was assigned a literal tire we had to carry every time we had physical training. These tires weren't moped tires; they were truck tires—huge and heavy and cumbersome and the absolute last thing anyone would want to carry while also exercising.

When we got into trouble—which seemed to happen often, even though it didn't seem like we'd done anything wrong—we were forced to hold our tires over our heads for several minutes. (If that doesn't sound difficult to you, try it.)

In addition to the strenuous and nonstop physical activity, target practice, driving practice, and learning defense tactics, we also had to cram two years' worth of studying the law somewhere into our days. Everything was scheduled to the minute, and no minutes were ever wasted. If they were, then we were probably holding our tires above our heads in the immediate aftermath.

We began with forty-five recruits. Within a month, ten had quit.

During boot camp, I learned how to be an officer—at least as much as I could learn while still in the relative safety of training. But I also learned two invaluable lessons that have always carried me through my work as an officer.

First, our instructors taught us never to give up, no matter the odds. When you give up on the street, you're dead. An officer can't afford to give up. The stakes are far too high. In hindsight, I now know that's why they were so hard on us in boot camp. They were preparing us for the real life-and-death battles we'd soon be facing on our own on the streets of Atlanta.

Second, the academy drilled into us how essential teamwork is to being a police officer. Many of the trainees in my class already had a deep understanding of that necessity; they'd served in the military. Several had been Army Rangers or Special Forces. One had even been a Navy diver. These service members knew that teamwork keeps you alive. Many of them had just returned home from battle overseas. I would learn so much from them.

As we endured boot camp together, we leaned on each other's strengths. And when those strengths became a unified front, we felt unstoppable. I learned how to trust and rely on my brothers and sisters in the force.

Never give up.

Always trust your team.

These lessons have kept me alive in many harrowing circumstances.

CHAPTER 14

ROOKIE

GRADUATING from the DeKalb County police academy was a great accomplishment for me. I felt as if I'd done something purposeful and meaningful. For the first time in some time, I was proud of myself for having set a goal and achieved it.

And, looking back, I was glad to join the brotherhood of law enforcement. Maybe, in some way, my new police family would help ease the pain of having lost my brother and father just a few years before.

I was also ecstatic to be done with training for many reasons. I wouldn't have to drag a tire at least once a day. I didn't feel as if my days were so full that I couldn't have a thought to myself. And, most of all, I hoped that my schedule would change for the better.

In scary echoes of my father and mother's relationship right before they divorced, my schedule at the academy was hurting my marriage with Nicol. I simply wasn't available. I would train at the academy from 7 a.m. to at least 6 p.m. Then—because I still owned that restaurant—I'd sometimes have to head there after my training and help close the store.

For all the time I was gone, Nicol was at home with our new baby girl, in addition to taking care of Hannah when she was with us. Still, despite these burdens of solo-parenting during those long days, Nicol fought through it. She was happy that I was finally getting a steady paycheck every two weeks *and* that we finally had good health benefits for our entire family. In other words, she knew we all had to make sacrifices so that our future could be better than our past.

I was ready, willing, and anxious to hit the streets and test myself. Would the skills I'd learned and honed over the previous eight months hold up in real-life situations? I wanted to know.

But the department doesn't just send out new recruits by themselves (thank God). I was assigned a field training officer for my first eight weeks of official duty to ensure I was ready to be a full-time police officer for the DeKalb County force.

After eight weeks where I acquitted myself of my duties adequately enough, I was released from field training and allowed to cover my beat alone. Rookie officers tend to get the evening shifts, so I worked from 4 p.m. to 2 a.m. This new shift was both a blessing and a curse.

Nicol appreciated these hours more than when I'd attended the academy. At least I could be home during the day to watch the kids. She could even have time to work out because she didn't have to watch the kids all day. Plus, my beat was close to home, so my commute was minimal. I could even drop by the house most nights for dinner and to kiss my kids goodnight.

However.

Nicol and I were still two ships passing in the night—well, in the late afternoon. We felt like we rarely saw each other unless it was for some practical reason. A date night hadn't happened for months. I could feel our relationship stretching thin, but neither of us knew what to do about it. We knew sacrifices had to be made, but I don't think either of us wanted to sacrifice our marriage.

Still, any marriage can't last long when quality time fades to nothing.

In the moments when I despaired that our relationship was fragile enough to break, I recalled my academy training.

Never give up.

Always trust your team.

I wouldn't give up on us, and I would trust her—and God—that we could get through this season.

CHAPTER 15

MOVIE FIGHT

LIKE ANY OFFICER who's worked on the force for longer than a few months, I have my war stories and the faces I'll never forget.

I worked that evening shift for almost four years. It was one of the hardest shifts because we'd receive most of the accidents from the five o'clock rush hour as well as the more intense crimes that always seemed to happen under the cover of darkness.

Shortly after my untethering from the field training officer, I was dispatched to a domestic abuse situation around 10 p.m. An adult child who suffered from bipolar disorder was off of his medications and beating his mother.

I was the first officer to arrive on the scene. As I opened my car door, I heard screams coming from a third-floor apartment. I keyed my mic and requested immediate backup.

I ran up the stairs, screams leading my way toward apartment #4.

My mic crackled. "Officer Turner, this is Dispatch. Backup isn't available at this time. Too many calls."

I keyed my mic twice to acknowledge. As soon as I did, I heard my sergeant's voice over the mic. "I'll be your backup, Turner." I keyed my mic twice again, grateful that backup would be on the way.

But the screams continued.

I quickly weighed my options: *Do I wait for backup—that I most likely need—or do I face the danger of this situation on my own?*

Officers don't always have the benefit of time. My adrenaline was high, but I knew I needed to do my job, and that was to help the person who called no matter the sacrifice.

I checked the door handle and found it locked. I knocked. "This is Officer Turner with the DeKalb County PD. Open the door, now." I was loud, forceful, and in command.

A few seconds later, the door opened.

A looming black male in his mid-twenties stood before me, blood dripping from his hands. I saw an older woman a few feet behind him: the mother I'd heard screaming for the last few minutes.

Her head was dripping red.

I barked at the suspect, "Get on the ground, slowly. Spread your hands as wide as you can."

He gave me a blank stare and then attempted to shut the door in my face.

I stuck my foot out to prevent its closing, then I forced the door open and grabbed the suspect by the arm. We wrestled back outside into the hallway, fighting each other for leverage. I just wanted to get him on the ground, but he wouldn't relent.

Eventually, we fought each other to the brink of the steps leading to the second floor. Then, as if we'd been in a scripted fight for some cop movie, the two of us tumbled down the stairs, locked in a battle I wanted to end as soon as I could.

We rolled down three flights of stairs. I threw punches and jabs wherever I could.

At the bottom, the both of us dazed and confused by our sudden stop, the suspect took that moment of freedom to sprint away.

But he didn't know how unrelenting I was either. I gave chase. (Never give up!) I keyed dispatch to let them know where I was headed, toward an adjacent apartment complex.

Then I saw this young man, with seemingly no effort, jump up and over a ten-foot-tall fence topped with barbed wire and into a neighboring complex. (It wouldn't be the last time I'd witness suspects surging with adrenaline accomplishing near superhuman feats during their escape.)

As I stood on the opposite side of the fence from my still-sprinting suspect, I saw my sergeant's car pull into the parking lot across from me. In just a few moments, my sergeant had caught the suspect.

Again, it felt like a movie. How in the world did my sergeant show up at just the right place at just the right time? But I didn't worry much about that at the time. I was just glad that the fight and subsequent chase—which may have lasted ten minutes but felt like it'd taken an hour—were over.

I took more than a few deep breaths and pulled myself together before driving to the opposite parking lot to pick up my suspect.

My body ached all over, I was scratched from head to toe, and I could feel a goose egg welling up on the back of my head from where I'd struck the railing while on our epic stairwell fight.

Once back in my patrol car, with the suspect in my rear seat, I felt my own adrenaline high subside. Suddenly, I was supremely tired.

I walked the suspect into the jail as my fellow officers cajoled me with, "What happened to you, Rook?"

I just smiled as I thought, *Welcome to the real world— not academy life.*

Once I'd taken care of the paperwork from that call and apprehension, I still had two hours left on my shift. I could have asked off just to recuperate. But I didn't want to be the rookie cop who couldn't handle himself, and I didn't want my teammates having to pick up my slack.

I had a job to do, and I wasn't going to let my first truly challenging call prevent me from doing it.

CHAPTER 16

SHOTS FIRED

ON ANOTHER MEMORABLE night for all the wrong reasons, I was out on patrol in a neighborhood that had been experiencing a constant barrage of burglaries, robberies, and car break-ins.

As I drove around the neighborhood, I spotted an older-model car circling the same street. His right tail light was out, so I drove slowly behind him while I ran his plates to see if the car belonged to anyone in the neighborhood.

I then chose to initiate a traffic stop to talk to the driver. As I was just about to turn on my blue lights, the driver began heading away from the neighborhood and toward the interstate.

I must have been made.

I flicked my lights on, but the driver refused to stop. Now, what could have been just a tail-light infraction had turned into something much more costly for this would-be suspect.

Surprisingly, the driver didn't seem to be trying to outrun me. Even though he'd gotten onto the interstate, his speed topped out at fifty-five miles per hour—a strange occurrence for someone who surely seemed like he was trying to get away.

But his comparatively slow speed made sense for what was about to happen.

After trailing him for just a quarter of a mile, I keyed dispatch. "I've got a driver refusing to stop on 285 Northbound and Indian Creek. I'm giving chase."

I released the radio's handle then heard the unmistakable sound of gunfire.

Time slowed as pop-pop-pop rattled around me.

I saw the driver's side of the suspect's car light up as his muzzle flashed with each successive shot.

And since I'd had my driver's side window halfway down, I could smell the gunpowder.

Though that experience took less than a couple of seconds, it felt like an eternity.

Then time snapped back to reality when a bullet struck my windshield—the closest any shot's ever come to my head.

I ducked out of an immediate reaction to imminent danger, but I kept up my pursuit.

The suspect kept firing. He hurled multiple rounds in my direction.

The other cars in my vicinity hit their brakes, trying as best as they could to avoid getting hit by gunfire. I prayed they'd be safe.

Then I prayed *I'd* be safe.

I'd been following from behind, both of us in the middle lane. When he started firing, I positioned my car to the far right rear of his vehicle, meaning that I was halfway in the right lane, forcing him to shoot out his back window to target me.

Which, of course, he did.

For reasons I'd never know, he seemed to really want me dead.

With my eyes straight ahead and all my senses heightened, I keyed dispatch again. "Shots fired. Send backup ASAP."

The chase carried on for another mile until we approached an exit and I saw my salvation in my rear view mirror: the flashing blue lights of DeKalb County PD cruisers. And, not only were they behind me, I also saw a few ahead of me, entering the interstate from the entry ramp.

Unsurprisingly, the suspect began shooting *at them* as well.

I prayed yet again for my fellow officers to make it out of this alive.

Suddenly, like a scene from *Dukes of Hazzard*, the suspect made a hard right, jumped the guardrail, and became stuck on the median.

I stopped a safe distance away and exited my car, gun drawn. I didn't know what to expect, but other officers were also approaching the suspect. Together, we were strong, and we would apprehend this violent suspect.

As I approached his now-defunct car, I saw a young black man with a shaved head lying unconscious with blood running down his forehead. He didn't seem to be moving —at all.

As I kept cautiously nearing him, I finally understood what had happened.

He'd shot himself.

Upon closer inspection, I saw that the suspect wore a shoulder holster and had several handguns and multiple boxes of ammunition within his car. I thought, *No wonder he could keep shooting. He has an arsenal in here.*

I also realized, with grave acknowledgment that most

law enforcement officers are shot during otherwise routine traffic stops, *If he would have stopped when I'd flashed my lights and I would have gotten out of my car to ask him a few simple questions, it's likely he would have killed me as soon as I approached him.*

I said a quick prayer of thanks, both for my own safety and those of my fellow officers. For all the shots that had been fired, only one had been deadly.

I later learned that the suspect had been out on parole for child molestation charges. He shouldn't have had guns in his possession either. I'm still not sure why he killed himself. Likely, he didn't want to go back to prison.

I certainly believe that my guardian angel was watching over me that night. I went home and hugged Mary, Hannah, and Nicol, who was then pregnant with our daughter, Jamie. I thanked God for them. I was grateful to be allowed more time with them.

And I felt as if I were given my first proper glimpse into the real-world consequences of this job.

Death was always on the line.

CHAPTER 17

ROOKIE MISTAKE

THE CALL that almost killed me happened at the end of one of my shifts. By chance, I happened to spot a tow truck that had been reported as stolen by a few close community friends of mine.

I followed the truck and told dispatch I was doing so. But, since it was between shift changes, they warned me that no other units would be available to assist.

I may have thought, *How come I always pick shift changes to start chases?*

I initiated a traffic stop. Fortunately, the truck pulled into a nearby parking lot.

But, as soon as I stopped, he took off.

I thought, *This again? Really?*

Then I may have laughed. Seconds after the tow truck had tried to escape, it died. The suspect tried to restart the engine, but all I heard was that noticeable startup grind. He wasn't going anywhere.

But I knew better than to think this was going to be an ordinary traffic stop. There are no ordinary traffic stops until *after* the stop has been completed and the suspect has either been let go or apprehended.

Sure enough, the suspect jumped out of the truck and sprinted across the street to a nearby apartment complex.

I got back into my car and gave chase. I parked at the complex's entrance, then chased the suspect on foot around the nearest building.

As I edged around a corner, I saw the suspect attempting to climb a ten-foot fence.

I pulled my gun. "Come down, now!"

He complied, but then he ran back toward where we'd just been.

As I gave chase, I holstered my gun and drew my Taser.

I rounded a corner and saw the—*Oh no. What a rookie mistake. And I'm not even a rookie anymore.*

He was climbing into a waiting car with an open driver's side door.

My car.

My *running* car.

Somehow, I was able to get to him before he could shift into drive. I tried to dislodge my keys with my left hand while striking the suspect on the head with my right fist several times.

But I failed.

The suspect dropped my cruiser into drive and hit the gas at full speed.

The only problems were that I was still halfway out of the car and four-foot-tall retaining walls surrounded us.

I was soon carried over one of those walls.

When my feet came out from underneath me, I fell onto my back on the solid asphalt. When the back of the vehicle then came over the wall, the open driver's side door pinned me to the ground. Then the car dragged me for another twenty feet until that open door shut, which released me from its terrifying hold.

As I watched my stolen squad car being driven away, I laid there in shock. *How did I not just die?*

Eventually, I picked myself up and inspected the damage. I was scraped from head to toe, but the wounds seemed superficial. However, my abdomen was swelling. I knew I'd have to get that checked at least.

An ambulance arrived and transported me to the nearest hospital. After an evaluation, nothing had been broken—aside from my pride.

I later heard that the suspect had dumped my patrol vehicle at a car wash about five miles away from our altercation. Other units had searched that area, but they never found the suspect.

Investigations worked hard over the next several weeks showing me photo lineups of possible suspects, but none of them looked like the suspect. After a while, the case went cold. (If, by chance, the suspect ever reads this book, just know you will pay for what you did at some point.)

My years on the streets included more shots being fired in my direction, fights, and foot and car chases. I even got into an altercation with a drug addict who stabbed me in the hand with a used syringe. I had to get tested for AIDS and hepatitis for a year. Despite all of this, I don't regret daily putting on the uniform.

Through all of it, I think my dad and brother were watching and protecting me every time I hit the streets.

CHAPTER 18

DETECTIVE TURNER

AFTER FOUR YEARS of patrolling the streets of Atlanta, I enrolled in prerequisite investigative classes so I could take the criminal investigation test required to become a detective. I passed on my first try and was promptly promoted to detective in our elite Major Felony Unit.

This division handled all of the major crimes, from robberies to homicides. Consequently, it was the hardest to get into. I was proud of the day I was promoted and excited to start something new.

I also believed that I could make a direct difference in people's lives. I thought the new posting might even help me find closure with my father's murder.

Just as when I'd become a patrolman, the department partnered me with a more experienced detective to show me the ropes. We were mainly assigned to robbery cases, from run-of-the-mill personal robberies to large-scale business robberies.

Because our caseload was heavy, we were also cross-trained to handle assaults and homicides. I was glad to do so because that meant I'd learn to work crime scenes and conduct interviews and interrogations.

Solving a robbery is harder than solving most cases. The success percentage is low for a number of reasons. Mainly, most robberies happen under the cover of night. All too often, victims can't identify suspects because they'd never adequately seen what the suspects looked like—if they'd seen the suspects at all.

That's where one of my academy lessons revealed itself to be true yet again: always trust your team. With each successive robbery I worked, I'd witness a consistent theme. It didn't happen all of the time, but we solved many cases because the first responders to a robbery call had seen or even apprehended the suspects on their arrival at the scene of the crime.

Good policing on the streets means knowing your community. My fellow officers were good police. When the suspect wasn't caught in the immediate aftermath of a robbery, they knew how to gather good leads.

I paid attention to their methods and tried my best to follow suit. As I became more experienced and more accomplished, I felt that I was actually good at interviewing suspects. In fact, I felt as if I were often able to get them to confess.

However, interviewing the victims became emotionally draining. Too many of the robberies I worked involved at least one victim who'd been shot. They'd often be taken to Grady Memorial Hospital, which has one of the best trauma units in the country. I spent more hours than I can remember entering their automatic doors and heading to the nearest recovery room to speak to a recently shot victim. I felt terrible for them and silently wished we could have gotten to them before their lives had been altered by violence.

But robberies didn't keep me busy back then. Homicides did. Even though I was assigned to robberies, our homicide rate was much higher at the time. Consequently, I was often tagging along to a murder scene.

I appreciated the challenge of these cases and being allowed to conduct more detective work. I also thought that my past experience as a homicide victim's family member would help me be a better detective. I could see portions of myself—my confusion, my anger, my grief—in the face of every family member who'd suddenly and unexpectedly lost their loved one.

For the rest of this chapter and the next, consider yourself warned: these true-life stories are gruesome. I relate them now to reveal the aftereffects of evil actions I saw all too often.

All the detectives worked together and were assigned different tasks on each homicide. Because I was a new detective, my main responsibilities, early on, at a homicide scene were to secure and canvass the area for witnesses. Eventually, I was assigned the body—to do all the drawings and victimology.

I'll never forget the first homicide scene I worked with those responsibilities.

Someone had called in that they'd found the body of their friend. Because they hadn't talked to that friend in several days, they'd gone into her residence to check on her.

I opened the door to the quiet residence and couldn't

believe what I saw: a slow trickle of blood was coming through the kitchen ceiling.

I walked upstairs and saw the victim: a woman in her thirties lying half-naked in a pool of her own blood. Multiple stab wounds pockmarked her chest and arms.

I was so taken aback by the scene that I momentarily forgot my responsibilities. All I could think was, *How angry does someone have to be to do something like this?* Several emotions then flooded my brain. I shook my head to clear my mind. *Your job, Turner, is to find who did this. So let's focus on that.*

Eventually, we caught the culprit. He's serving life in prison.

After working several homicide cases, one memorable case —for all the wrong reasons—fell into my lap. It began as a robbery and resulted in a homicide.

What made it comparatively worse than the other cases I'd worked is that I knew the victim.

A call came into dispatch to any available officers to assist with a robbery that had just happened at a package store. I immediately knew where it was located; that package store had been on my beat when I was a patrolman. In fact, I'd gotten to know the owners well because I used to check on them at night when they were closing shop. I wanted to ensure they got into their car safely.

They were a kind Vietnamese couple who'd moved to the area thirty years ago. They had no money, but they somehow found a way to seek the American dream. In time, they opened that package store, raised two kids—both of whom they put through college—and, last I'd heard, they were getting ready to sell the business so they could retire.

When I heard the name of their store, I feared the worst.

During my investigation, I learned that the suspect had entered the store and struck the store owner several times over the head with a blunt object.

The store owner fell to the floor, unconscious.

The suspect stole the cash register and fled.

A customer came into the store ten minutes later and saw the owner lying on the ground—breathing, but just barely. The customer called 911, and that's when the call went out that I'd heard.

The victim had lost a lot of blood from the traumatic blow to his head. He was rushed to a nearby hospital. He never regained consciousness. After a week, he died.

I was furious that such a good person had been killed for maybe a few hundred dollars.

I worked hard to find his killer, but the case had no leads. The store had no security cameras. There'd been no witnesses, even of the suspect fleeing the scene. Those who'd searched the crime scene found nothing either. After months of investigating, the case went cold.

I felt terrible for the victim's wife and family, fearing they'd never have closure. I also learned the sad fact that the store owner and his wife had found a buyer for their store. They had been scheduled to turn the business over just two weeks after the owner had met his untimely and unwarranted end.

But, closure did arrive, although it took seven years to do so. By then, the suspect was in jail, and he was bragging to another inmate about how he'd beaten an Asian man to death at a local package store.

I couldn't believe his callousness, but I shouldn't have been surprised. At least the victim's family could have some measure of closure.

But, as one who'd long expected closure regarding my own father's death, even though we knew who'd done it and why, I knew it wouldn't be enough.

Answers don't resurrect people.

After working and assisting in hundreds of homicide, robbery, and assault cases, the work began affecting me on a deep level. I looked in the mirror one day and realized I'd become someone different than when I'd started on the force.

Maybe I should have expected that, but I didn't like who I'd become.

Then I worked the most horrific case of my career.

CHAPTER 19

OVER AND OUT

I'D WORKED multiple homicides and had seen far too many dead bodies, but I still wasn't prepared for what I saw and experienced on a cold November evening.

Before arriving at the crime scene, I'd been briefed by a patrol officer that the initial call had come from the victim's husband. He'd arrived home around 8 p.m. to find his wife dead. His children had also been killed.

With that information, I tried to steel my resolve before entering the home. But as soon as I saw the scene, I realized how pointless that was. No one could have prepared themselves to see what I saw that night.

I first saw the man's wife next to a staircase. She was facedown in her own blood, her head bashed in. I carefully walked by her lifeless body and up the stairs to the nursery. Her two children were in cribs, also lying in pools of their own blood. Neither child seemed older than two. It appeared that their heads had been bashed in by a blunt object.

From my initial assessment, it surely looked as if the same murder weapon had been used on all three victims.

I felt myself getting sick, both to my stomach and to my soul. *How does something like this happen?* I'd asked myself that question at hundreds of crime scenes, but, if you're a detective long enough, there are always cases that are more horrific than others.

The husband—already my prime suspect—was transported to headquarters for further questioning while we investigated the scene of the crime. During his interview, it became quite clear quite quickly that the man's story simply did not add up. After several hours of being interrogated, the husband confessed to killing his wife and two young boys.

Why? Why? Why!

The man said his wife had threatened to leave him and take their children—so he'd chosen to kill them. After beating his wife to death, he'd murdered his children while they were asleep.

The investigation took all night and into the early morning hours. The man took us to a nearby daycare center dumpster where he'd tossed his bloody clothes and his murder weapon: a claw hammer.

But the trash had already been picked up by then. We figured out what dump truck had removed the contents and located it. Along with three other detectives, I spent several hours sorting through tons of garbage. Eventually, we found several bloody towels, his bloody clothes, and his bloody murder weapon.

As I looked at the evidence I held in my hands and considered what this man had done to his family not less than twenty-four hours ago, I wanted to accost the suspect. I wanted to grab him and shake him and yell at him, "What gives you the right to take the life of another human being—and especially the lives of defenseless children *in their beds?*"

I didn't feel sorry for the suspect.

That case went to court, but the suspect received life in prison.

I thought cases like that are why the death penalty should exist.

When I was a new detective, a senior detective warned me: "Don't hug on the family due to the loss of their loved one because then you become emotionally involved. After you work a hundred of these cases, it will start to affect you mentally."

He was right.

When I'd first started as an investigator, I knew I was going to be great because I could empathize with the victims. I'd been in their exact shoes. But, after less than a hundred cases, I quickly learned that a robbery and homicide detective can't show weakness.

My weakness was that I cared.

In time, the job did wear me down. How could it not?

Instead of caring—for the victims, for my family, for myself—I allowed a hard shell to form around me. Nothing would bother me. Instead of showing emotion, I remained rational. I lived in my head and told my heart to quit feeling. My job was to solve cases—nothing more, nothing less.

Eventually, of course, the way I handled myself at work became the way I handled myself at home. And the long hours required of me at my job meant that I wasn't even home that often. Tensions were high nearly anytime I was home with Nicol. To augment our frustrations, we could never plan even a simple date night because it seemed that I'd get called away on a moment's notice.

Plus, most of the time I was home, I just wanted to rest. I was physically, emotionally, and mentally drained.

Then, one night, while sitting on my couch and wondering why my life was this way, I figured something drastic needed to change. My family needed the old Jeremy back, the one who was a good husband and father, and the one who was actually home—physically, emotionally, and mentally. I didn't want to keep living the same life we'd endured for the last four years. I didn't want to hide within my protective shell any longer too.

The next day, I asked my supervisor for a transfer to the fraud or burglary unit, someplace with less stress and less on-call time. He understood my desire and agreed to grant my transfer, but I had to wait two months for a position to become available.

Those two months would forever change my life.

PART 5

ICP

CHAPTER 20

POPCORN AND WATER

WHEN I WAS STILL A PATROLMAN, I was once dispatched to assist the Department of Family and Children Services with a welfare check on five kids. I thought, *Five? That can't be good.*

My intuition would prove correct.

I knocked on the apartment door.

A girl who might have been nine tentatively cracked open the door. Her dirty clothes hung off her like rags. She clutched an old doll in her left hand. She looked at me without saying a word, equal parts fear and hope in her eyes.

In my nicest voice, I asked, "Where's your mommy?"

"She's not home."

I paused to see if she'd tell me more, but she'd answered the question. She probably had no clue where her mom was. I shuddered to think how often this little girl must have thought, *Where is my mommy?*

"May I come in? I need to check on you and your brothers and sisters."

She opened the door wide and confronted me with the brutal reality of poverty.

Immediately, I saw the other four children, all younger than the girl who'd answered the door. They looked just as dirty and downcast as the girl.

Their "furniture" was comprised of several blankets on the floor. Power cords trailed like snakes throughout the room, terminating in the laundry room *outside* of the apartment's front door. They wound their way to a microwave in the kitchen and a lamp elsewhere. I couldn't believe what I was seeing.

"Hey, kids. Have you all eaten dinner yet?"

The nine-year-old answered, "We've had some popcorn and water."

Unbelievable. These poor kids.

Their caseworker had previously told me that the children's mother had been leaving them alone several evenings per week. The caseworker would often check on them. When she received my call, the caseworker attempted to reach the mother one last time. But the mom couldn't be reached.

Which meant I had to take the children to a group home.

I tried to explain what was happening and what was going to happen, but home is home. They didn't want to be taken away. They wailed.

"Everything's going to be OK," I promised. "You'll see. You're going to a place with actual beds and hot food. You'll get more than popcorn and water, I promise."

I'm not sure they believed me. They were just sad.

So was I.

When I think about what prompted me to do more than

just police work—which I love doing and which needs to be done—I think about this story.

I still see that nine-year-old girl believing that popcorn and water was a meal.

CHAPTER 21

MY INTERACTIVE CALLING

DURING THE TWO months I waited to be transferred to a less stressful division than robberies and homicides, our chief started a new unit: the Interactive Community Police. The ICP unit would interact with citizens to help the community solve neighborhood problems. Think of it as a unit established to build goodwill into the community while simultaneously trying as hard as possible to solve systematic problems that plagued our neighborhoods, like home-lessness.

When I heard about the new unit, I jumped at the chance to join. Their intentions and purpose closely aligned with where I felt God leading me. Author and theologian Frederick Buechner wrote, "The place God calls you to is the place where your deep gladness and the world's deep hunger meet."[1] My deep gladness to help people through tough times was about to meet the world's deep hunger.

I didn't know it at the time, but being hired into the ICP was the beginning of my deeper calling. I was fortunate to receive the position as well. Several hundred had applied. The benefits were great too. We received excellent training, a take-home car, and I was assigned to the precinct where I lived. Not only would my commute be decreased, but I would also be serving the people of my neighborhood.

Plus, maybe best of all (if I'm being selfish), I worked four days a week and had the weekends off. I couldn't remember the last time I'd had weekends off. This meant I could spend more time with my family, something all of us had long desired. I didn't have to be on call during the weekends either. It was freedom. The extra time allowed Nicol and I to better ensure the health of our relationship, which overflowed to better relationships with our kids. Time is love.

I thoroughly believe the old adage that when God closes one door, he opens another. He did for me. I like to think that he had other plans for me than working long hours, going to court, and seeing dead bodies every day. The job change to ICP made me healthier in all the ways I'd been failing. It felt as if the puzzle pieces of my life were beginning to fall into place.

Whenever someone asked me about my job, I'd tell them about a Norman Rockwell plate my mom had collected and displayed when I was young. The picture on the plate portrayed a police officer and a child who'd just run away from home. The boy's knapsack on a stick sits at his feet. The two of them are in an ice cream parlor, and the officer is slightly leaning over to the boy, obviously speaking with him. The boy is looking directly at the officer's eyes, paying attention. I imagine that the officer was asking the boy why he'd run away, whether he thought that was a good idea, and "How do you think your mom and dad feel right now?" And the boy is listening and considering his argument because the officer respects the boy—and will likely buy him some ice cream.

For the most part, officers don't do things like that anymore. But ICP was our start in Atlanta.

I loved my new gig from the get-go. I felt we'd needed a position like mine for ages, one where an officer is allowed to be proactive with the community instead of reactive to a crime. By default, my new job got me more involved in my community. I got to know many people who could use my help. Time and again, I got the opportunity to talk with people who just wanted to speak with an officer about making their neighborhood a better place.

Fortunately, the community liked our presence. Well, at least the people I routinely spoke to liked our presence. They also appreciated that if a problem arose, they had my cell number. Instead of calling police headquarters, they could contact me directly. I know a lot of people appreciated that small difference in how our unit functioned.

Soon after ICP began and we'd started hearing about ways the neighborhood needed help, one issue repeatedly came up. The drunks, panhandlers, perverts, or who-knows-what were ruining the community.

In other words, people in my neighborhood were tired of dealing with the homeless.

---

1. Frederick Buechner, *Wishful Thinking: A Seeker's ABC* (San Francisco: HarperOne, 1993).

CHAPTER 22

MY FRIEND JOE

I CAN STILL SEE myself as an elementary-school student sitting cross-legged and being asked, "What do you want to be when you grow up?"

I'd often say fireman or lawyer. I never said police officer.

In a similar vein, I never heard any of my classmates say, "I want to be homeless" or "I want to be a drug addict."

Whenever I saw the homeless in my community, I would often think about my childhood classmates. None of these homeless adults had *aspired* to homelessness. As an officer, I had learned over and over that life doesn't always go the way you want it to.

Heck, I'd learned that in my own life just as many times.

Inevitably, life doesn't go as planned. In the meantime, the best thing we can do is to help each other.

That's why I was thrilled to be part of the ICP in my very own community. I was being paid to help people who wanted and needed help. And our homeless population needed help.

When I was a patrolman, I'd gotten to know many of the homeless by name. Likewise, they knew me as Jeremy—not Officer Turner. I tried to bring these homeless friends of mine something to eat or drink if I knew I would see them on a given day. I hoped that my meager offerings would brighten their day, even if momentarily.

But, for the people on the streets who didn't know me and my heart, they saw the uniform and the badge before they saw me. They were unsure about trusting me. I couldn't blame them though. Many of them had past experiences with the police. After all, most of the time when somebody like me showed up to where they lived, that meant they were about to be taken to jail.

Had I been in their shoes, I would have been skeptical too. *What's that cop doing coming over here?*

I didn't let their doubt deter me though. In fact, I became good friends with many of the homeless, and particularly a homeless man named Joe who would become my go-between—my homeless community liaison.

He'd lived under a bridge in Atlanta for fifteen years by the time I'd met him. Consequently, he was knowledgeable about his community. He educated me about the ways they lived, and he would tell me about the people who'd pass through his "neighborhood." Mostly, Joe spoke with others like him and let them all know that I was an officer who could be trusted. He let them know that I visited so I could help, not so I could take them away.

During my first few months with ICP, I routinely came into contact with homeless people. It seemed as if I met more and more with each passing day. When I was on shift, I saw Joe every day. I think he liked having a new friend around to talk to, and I enjoyed talking to him. I learned so much about his life and what it must be like living on the streets full-time.

I realized that homelessness wasn't so much the problem; it was the inevitable result of greater problems. Most of the homeless people I dealt with suffered from a mental health affliction, alcohol addiction, drug addiction, or some toxic concoction of all three.

They were people in desperate need of help, and I desperately wanted to help them.

PART 6

CONTRIBUTE2AMERICA

CHAPTER 23

A SIMPLE VISION

I STILL CAN'T FULLY EXPLAIN what happened to me during one otherwise uneventful night on shift during my duties with ICP.

I felt the power of God overwhelm me. I was granted a simple vision that I needed to do more to help the needy in my community. It was as if my long-lost father and brother were talking to me, jointly molding a plan for my future.

A peace I hadn't experienced—maybe ever—overtook my soul.

I've written about hearing my calling before, but that was the moment I literally *heard my calling*. When I came down from that spiritual high, I realized what I was supposed to do.

The next day, I called my friend Tad, a local firefighter I'd known for six years. I knew that he wouldn't think what I'd experienced the night before was too strange.

At least, I hoped he wouldn't.

We met that day and I relayed how I felt impressed to start a nonprofit that would help the homeless in Atlanta by providing them with food, medical care, and other resources they needed.

Without hesitation, Tad smiled and said, "I'm in."

I smiled back, grateful for this first acknowledgment that what I was feeling led to do wasn't ridiculous or crazy. In time, more people would offer their help too. As an officer who worked in his own community, I'd formed many relationships over the years, out of necessity and nicety, that would provide the support I needed while forming my nonprofit. Many of my friends and neighbors pledged their help, whether through monetary donations, their time, or their resources.

And it was easy for them to jump in because I'd have immediate clientele. I'd heard about the needs of our homeless population for months, both directly from Joe and through other organizations like the United Way and the Salvation Army. I knew that what I had planned in my mind could provide real, tangible, immediate help to dozens, if not hundreds, of Atlanta-area homeless people.

I was anxious to get started, but I knew that forming a nonprofit was not just a matter of stating that I was going to do so and then signing a few papers to make it legal.

First, I needed to know if what I was planning to do wasn't already being done. I knew that some issues weren't being taken care of because of my near-daily association with our homeless population. Part of ICP's work included bridge cleanups, which meant I routinely saw the poor state of the homeless camps. But I also got to see how their faces would light up when our ICP would provide assistance.

During this formation time, I also attended monthly meetings at the United Way. I collaborated with that agency and other area nonprofits so that, collectively, we could better assist the large homeless population in Atlanta.

I worked on a business plan and took notes from other nonprofits regarding their successes and failures. I wanted to do this right, and I knew that that meant taking my time before launching. On top of my ICP work and my responsibilities as a father and husband, I worked as hard as I could every day to make my dream become a reality.

Then, one night as I was leading a crime watch meeting, I saw a neighbor in attendance who I knew ran a successful business in Atlanta. I immediately thought, *He'll know the next practical step I need to take. I need to talk to him ASAP.*

I accosted him after the meeting, told him about my idea for a nonprofit, and he said he'd be happy to help me.

Yet again, these quick words of verbal confirmation from people who both had the means and the desire to help me continued to affirm my path.

I was going to start a nonprofit to help the homeless.

CHAPTER 24

UNREAL

THE SUCCESSFUL BUSINESSMAN I met with said that my nonprofit reminded him of The Atlanta Project, which had been started by former president Jimmy Carter and his associate, James Laney, in 1991. Despite my best efforts at research, I was unaware of this project. But, apparently, my plan shared similarities with The Atlanta Project. For my nonprofit, I'd planned to section Atlanta into six zones. We'd provide each zone with care once a week while getting the surrounding communities to help out in each zone.

He and I brainstormed multiple ways this could be put into practice. The wheels for my nonprofit were put into motion.

But what would we call it?

In honor of my late father and all the others-centered service he'd done throughout his life, I wanted to name my nonprofit Mission America. By 2009, that organization had been dissolved. But I soon learned that another organization had taken the name.

I came up with a few more names, but every one was

already taken. Finally, as a last-ditch effort, I searched for available domain names. I knew my nonprofit would need a website, so I figured a memorable domain name might also make for a memorable nonprofit name. Plus, in the back of my mind, I didn't want a name that was only local to Atlanta (e.g., Mission Atlanta) because I hoped to one day take my nonprofit to a national level.

After several weeks of getting nowhere, a friend of mine, Brian, gave me a list of possible nonprofit names that met two qualifications: they weren't listed in the directory of state-registered corporations and they weren't already registered as a domain name.

The first entry was Contribute2America.

As soon as I read that, I told my friend that our search was over. The name was perfect.

I immediately contacted another close friend, Michael, a corporate attorney, and asked him to set up my new nonprofit, Contribute2America. Since I'd told him about my idea prior to this call (and maybe since our daughters were good friends), he did all the legal work for free. (When you're a nonprofit, it's very helpful to have helpful friends.)

My next challenge—and anyone who's ever launched a nonprofit knows where this is going—was filing for my nonprofit status with the IRS. I contacted Shane, another good friend and a CPA, to help. (Shane would eventually become C2A's CFO.)

For those unfamiliar with the process of becoming a legal nonprofit in America, the most challenging aspect is assessing your projected financial path and showing that to the IRS. How can you know how you'll support your nonprofit when you haven't even launched it? Let's just say I was *very* grateful for Shane's help during this time. Without likely boring you further, the process took six months, but we were finally approved as a registered nonprofit on 2009.

With governmental approval, we were ready and more than willing to take donations. My wife Nicol spearheaded several fundraisers for Contribute2America, including a wine-tasting event, live music at Smith's Old Bar, multiple silent auctions, and a fun run. I stood in front of Atlanta-area businesses asking for donations. I also placed C2A donation boxes at several businesses around town.

We also—of course—launched our website at Contribute2America.org. For those who wouldn't or couldn't discover us online, we created brochures too.

After that whirlwind of activity, I remember taking a moment to breathe. Even though we'd been working hard for months to make this nonprofit real, it still felt as if it didn't really exist—like it was just a figment of my imagination, a fever dream that was never really meant to come true.

But when I saw our website and those brochures, I thought, *This looks legit!*

I also thought, *I never want someone to take this name.* Soon after, I contacted a neighbor who just so happened to be a trademark attorney—as if God knew all the pieces I would need to make this puzzle complete. Mike provided the trademarking process for me for free, and he added the bonus service of defending us in court should anyone ever try to use our nonprofit name—also for free. I was gladdened to know that we'd be covered if that would happen to us.

The last piece of the puzzle (before we actually began the real work at C2A) fell into place when yet another friend, who happened to be a local property manager, allowed us to use an open office space for free in one of his vacant buildings. However, there was one caveat: the office needed some work.

Well, I knew how to do that.

I gladly accepted the offer, then promptly went to our new office space to see what needed to be done. Soon after, we painted the walls and put new carpet in.

Contribute2America had a headquarters.

With the legal work complete, the website running, and the office ready for us to work, I felt a sense of broad accomplishment I hadn't felt since graduating from the academy. But this time was different because of the many people who'd directly helped me bring my vision to reality. I could never repay them for all the ways they'd each contributed to the cause, but I could thank them.

Once the headquarters were open, I invited everyone who'd helped me get that far to visit at the same time, then I thanked them from the bottom of my heart for what they'd allowed me to do with their generosity in time, money, and service.

Contribute2America was ready to contribute to America.

Or at least Atlanta.

CHAPTER 25

THE WORK BEGINS

DURING CONTRIBUTE2AMERICA'S FIRST YEAR, we concentrated on an area east of Atlanta and the Peachtree Creek. Why did we start there?

The creek starts just northeast of Atlanta and runs west through the northern part of the city before finding its termination in the Chattahoochee River. Because the creek bisects the city of Atlanta (population: 486,290), it flows beneath dozens of bridges, and beneath those dozens of bridges lived dozens of Atlanta-area homeless people. Additionally, I also already knew many of these people because they'd been in my patrol territory.

Our first "event" as Contribute2America was simply Tad and me driving to these areas in my truck, with C2A magnets affixed to the exterior, finding anyone who could use a hand. We'd give them food, medical screenings, and wound-care management that included mostly cleaning rashes and cuts. We had two patients that day who needed to be rushed to the hospital due to high blood pressure; one suffered from liver disease and was in bad shape. We also provided socks, jackets, and blankets to those who needed them.

Now, I should have known that what happened next was going to happen. I'd developed trusting relationships with these people before officially launching C2A. I knew how the grapevine worked in these makeshift homeless villages.

Word traveled.

I could only imagine the incredulous discussions:

"Did you hear about that cop who's helping people like us?"

"What? You mean he's like just talkin' to us as normal people?"

"Ha. No. I mean, yeah, he is, but he's also givin' out stuff. Food and medical assistance. For free."

"Nah. You gotta be kiddin' me. Ain't no *cop* gonna come *help us* on his time off."

"It's true! Joe told me 'bout him just yesterday."

"Guess I'll have to go see it for myself then."

Soon enough, Tad and I were traveling to several bridges per week, and it seemed as if our crowds grew every week. I got to know even more of them by name, and they came to trust me. I think they even looked forward to seeing my truck pull up, knowing that we were bringing conversation as well as food and supplies.

Eventually, my name somehow found its way to the United Way, and they asked if they could partner with me in these bridge services. Since one of my foundational principles for C2A is that we can do more together than we can alone ("Always trust your team," right?), I readily agreed. I never wanted my nonprofit to be siloed, as if my team were the only ones who should be helping. The problems we faced were many times bigger than our fledgling nonprofit, so I was thrilled when the United Way asked to partner.

They had more resources for housing the homeless. They worked with several nonprofit agencies in the area but wanted to reach more by getting out of the office and hitting the streets—like I had been doing. They soon joined me on all of my bridge work and gave assistance to those who wanted to get out from under the bridge. The United Way would take them to hospitals for detox, and, when that was completed, the United Way would place them in housing and provide counseling and job placement.

As my routine clientele grew from helping ten people per month to helping fifty, I knew I needed to partner with even more nonprofits in the Atlanta area. I also wanted to expand our medical assistance capabilities.

Those two prayers would be answered in quick succession—and by the same person.

CHAPTER 26

DR. TURNER?

IN ATLANTA, Safe House helps the homeless but focuses on assisting victims of teen sex trafficking.

Now, I've seen a lot of horrific things in my time as an officer and in working with the homeless. From dead bodies to drug addicts, I've witnessed some of the worst results of evil that one person can inflict upon one another, or upon themselves. But nothing fills me with more righteous fury than seeing how sex trafficking victims seem to lose their souls because someone with just a little power and too much greed sold them out. I was grateful for the work that Safe House did and still does.

When I spoke to their director about partnering, he asked, "Could you guys use a medical trailer?"

"Yeah, as a matter of fact. It sure could help us. Why? You have one just sitting out back?"

He smiled. "We sure do."

I should have known better than to be sarcastic. Fortunately, Safe House's director wasn't being sarcastic in reply. He was being honest! They'd had a medical trailer donated to them, but they rarely used it. Their director saw the opportunity where it might be used on a regular basis, so he let   Contribute2America use it as often as we needed it. I was astounded and grateful.

Since the trailer hadn't been used in quite some time, I contacted my mother and Nicol to help me clean it and sort through the medical supplies that were still stocked within the trailer. Several long and cramped days later, the trailer was clean, properly stocked, and ready to roll. I knew where our first destination would be.

When our new (but slightly used) and near-gleaming medical missions trailer pulled up to the bridge where Joe lived, I saw joy light up his face. He was genuinely glad to see our nonprofit growing so quickly because he knew that it meant more help for him and his neighbors. And I'd like to think that he was happy to see me enjoying small successes in my new endeavor.

Until we'd received that trailer, we had mostly just provided food—a necessity, of course, but the people under the bridge needed medical care too. Now that we had the trailer, we could conduct health screenings.

We discovered several "patients" with broken bones and infected abrasions from living in rather squalid conditions. They tended to just suffer through their injuries because so few of them had health insurance. They wouldn't go to the hospital, even for injuries most people couldn't endure for an hour. As we conducted these screenings, we'd even come across people who needed immediate help, so we'd call for an ambulance to transport them to the nearest hospital.

I was glad we could help, but I felt terrible for the state these men and woman had found themselves in. As I'd done ever since I'd started C2A, I asked myself yet again, *What more can we do?*

Having the medical trailer allowed us to help more people. After three months of traveling to bridges in our designated area of help, we were offered the opportunity to provide food and medical care at an event at Georgia State University.

Hosted by the Atlanta Homeless Coalition, the large-scale event hoped to bring together all of the Atlanta-area homeless services. Due to the large amount of homeless who would attend, this event was set up as a one-stop shop for the homeless. They could get all the resources they needed to assist them under one roof: food, medical and dental assistance, counseling, IDs, and assistance with social security and housing, for example.

C2A was a small fish in a big pond then, but we provided a huge impact. What was nice is that we had the medical trailer outside, where most of the homeless had congregated, while most of the other organizations were located inside the athletic arena. This gave us a great opportunity to meet a lot of people in need of assistance. After the day ended, we'd fed more than fourteen hundred homeless men and women and had provided medical screenings. Ultimately, with help from Nicol, my mother, and Tad, we cared and fed more than two thousand people—the most we'd helped in such a short amount of time since C2A had begun.

In addition to doing the work we were called to do, I made a number of contacts with other homeless-assistance organizations in Atlanta. Our appearance at that event also placed us in a small category or organizations who knew how to help people in large numbers without needing to secure funding from larger nonprofits. In other words, we were a scrappy startup that could make a small budget work.

I think that's because I knew, personally, what it meant to make a small budget work. Not only was C2A still in its infancy as a nonprofit, but so was my experience in juggling my family life, my nonprofit work, and my other jobs.

Oh, did I fail to mention that I was still a full-time police officer during this time?

And, to make ends meet, I worked a few other part-time jobs, like security for the Centers for Disease Control and a local bank.

I was often devoting twenty hours per week to C2A, then another fifty hours to my paid work. I'm not complaining. But I am trying to paint a picture of the kinds of sacrifices that have to be made when launching and sustaining a nonprofit.

CHAPTER 27

WHAT MORE?

FOLLOWING the national fallout of the 2008 financial crisis, many families on my beat were forced out of their homes. With nowhere to go (unless they opted for their roof to be a bridge), these families wound up in extended stay motels usually located in high-crime areas. If you're unfamiliar with these often barely habitable places, they're motels that someone can rent not just by the night, but also by the week. They offer a roof, four walls, a place to sleep, and a bathroom, but it's still hard living.

I knew that from experience. I used to visit these motels all the time on calls for robberies, murders, fights, and drug deals gone bad. They seemed to be breeding grounds for illegal or violent behavior. I felt bad for the kids I often saw hiding behind doors, for the teenagers hanging out on the stairwells, and for all the single moms who seemed to populate these places.

In 2010, I was asked by a nonprofit called Pathway to connect with people living at extended stay motels and to assess how many people were living there. We had several such places in our county, but I wasn't aware of the actual number until I started this investigative work. All told, I visited twelve extended stay motels and was floored by the number of single mothers with children who were living there.

Most rooms had a double bed, meaning that all the family likely slept together. Their only appliances were a fridge and microwave. (I wondered how many of these kids would have considered popcorn and water a feast.) The kids ranged from newborns to seventeen-year-olds. In fact, I'd seen some of these extended-stay children at the schools when I'd done presentations on drugs and gangs.

In return for completing our survey, each extended-stay family was given a Target gift card. Once we'd compiled the information, we realized that a majority of these families qualified as homeless.

Although they might have had a temporary home above their heads on the day I'd spoken to them, they'd be out on the street the next night if they couldn't cough up their rent for that night or that week. In other words, they were living hand to mouth, with just enough to go on for the day ahead of them.

I knew this to be true from experience as well. I'd often find whole families sleeping in their cars in the parking lot because they couldn't pull together the money for one more night.

Even when I was exhausted from the work and the emotional toll that seeing such suffering can cause, a singular driving thought seldom left my mind: *I think we can always help more.*

CHAPTER 28

FEEDING THE HUNGRY

AFTER HAVING HELPED the homeless under the bridge for three years, I felt led to do more through Contribute2America. After conducting that survey for Pathway about people who lived in extended stay motels in Atlanta, I felt I could help them and others like them with groceries and other necessary resources, like assistance with utilities and transportation. But I wasn't sure how to go about doing that.

So, as I'd done before, I contacted someone who knew what they were doing. While I was trying to figure out just who that could be, someone at a monthly homeless outreach meeting told me to meet with pastor Chad Hale. He'd started a program out of his church called the Georgia Avenue Food Cooperative.

Soon thereafter, I met with Chad. He told me about the program he'd started many years before. What was funny to me is that Chad hadn't created the program out of thin air; he'd just copied the concept from a church in St. Petersburg, Florida. (For all he and I knew, *that* church might have copied from another church—or maybe it's just that feeding the hungry stemmed from a long tradition first spoken into existence by Jesus.)

The Georgia Avenue Food Cooperative provided a good amount of food to families on a monthly basis. It wasn't a one-and-done handout either. Families could rely on their monthly food assistance, which meant they could better budget their money since they wouldn't have to worry about a monthly food bill. This would allow them to use their money for rent, utilities, school, transportation, and many other necessities.

The program had a proven success rate in helping families get back on their feet, which meant that families didn't stay on the program forever. I think part of the program's success was due to the ownership its members felt. Every capable member of the Georgia Avenue Food Cooperative contributed their time, either by unloading the truck, organizing the food, or carrying food to be distributed. In other words, they helped themselves by helping each other.

I loved what Pastor Hale was doing, and I aimed to enact it in our area of Atlanta. But I'd need a home base larger than our headquarters. And our medical mission trailer certainly wouldn't be able to hold the amount of food we'd need to secure and keep for months on end.

I contacted another pastor I knew, Sondra Jones. She and I had worked on several projects before, and I thought her church would make for a great center point for families to meet at in order to get food. After I told Sondra what C2A wanted to do, she readily agreed to help. In fact, she'd been looking for more ways to reach out to her church's surrounding community. She saw our conversation as an answer to prayer.

Next, I set up C2A with the community food bank, which took about two months. The timeline was so long because the Atlanta Community Food Bank only sold food to nonprofits. To get their food, I had to fill out an application similar to the IRS nonprofit registration form. After reviewing my application, the Food Bank conducted a site visit. And, due to food safety regulations and the necessity of recording when the food was provided, I had to take several classes at the Food Bank in order to get approved.

Once all the pieces were in place to begin providing monthly food assistance, I began seeking out families who needed the kind of help we were now prepared to offer. I contacted a coworker of mine, Officer Jefferson, who routinely worked with all of the area schools. He put me in touch with a school counselor, someone who would know if a family was suffering due to a lack of food. The counselor referred ten families to me, and that number fit with our projected launch budget for this new aspect of C2A.

These first ten families were thrilled to have been chosen, especially after they were told exactly what they'd be receiving every month. Volunteers from Pastor Jones's church were equally excited about being able to help in such a tangible and consistent way. After several months, we added more families, who mostly arrived by referrals from families already in our cooperative or by referrals from the schools. In time, we were helping to support forty families with food every month.

I was glad that our growing nonprofit was doing more. I still thought we had more to do. But then I was reminded of the wise words of Brian who spoke this truth to me in so many words when I'd first started Contribute2America: "Launching is easy. Maintaining is hard."

I was four years into leading C2A. We were visiting and helping the homeless population under our bridges, we were providing medical care through our trailer, and we were offering forty families food every month. I was still working full-time as an officer, as well as working a few part-time jobs to make ends meet. And I was still, gratefully, a husband to a beautiful wife and a father to three great kids.

I finally realized, *Maintaining is hard. Maybe I should figure out a way where I can maintain what we have going with C2A before something crumbles.* As a result, I hired Reshane, an excellent secretary who, even though she worked part-time, made my life infinitely easier. She handled all the paperwork that accompanied running the food coop, she answered all of the office phone calls, she updated our website, she wrote and compiled our news-letter, and she did so much more. I was also glad to pay for Reshane to attend a certification program at Emory University to learn grant-writing so she could help C2A possibly land sometimes lucrative grants.

Unfortunately, my research failed to reveal any grants that would support exactly what we were about. Most grants are for specific needs, like counseling or housing—all good things, of course—but C2A's focus is often too broad to be considered for a grant. Plus, we're a first-responder type of organization, most often helping people in the streets, right where they are. Grants tend to be granted to organizations that have longer-lasting results, so to speak, like creating low-income housing. Consequently, in my nine years of running C2A, we've never received a government-funded grant.

But we carried on with fundraisers, and area churches and other foundations liked what we were doing. In fact, with the churches that already had some from of mission work they were about, they liked the possibility of working together with C2A to meet the needs of the people in their neighborhoods. Word kept spreading about who we were and our mission "to be a truly hands-on, face-to-face ally for those in need while empowering communities to make a lasting a difference."

Surprisingly, this would lead to recognition I could never have imagined happening.

CHAPTER 29

RECOGNITION AND EXPANSION

11ALIVE IS an Atlanta-area news station that, every year, picks eleven people from the community who are doing extraordinary work. In 2012, I was chosen as one of those eleven people.

My family and I attended a black-tie dinner to receive the prestigious award. I was treated like a hero all night, even though I didn't necessarily want the attention. But I knew that such attention on me meant more attention for Contribute2America, which meant more help for the people we served. I never started C2A for accolades; I started it because it was the right thing to do.

Just a couple of months later, I was awarded the CEO Award in DeKalb County for my community work. I was astounded to have won that as well. Winning was a cool experience, of course, but the dual recognition so close together placed my small nonprofit into the same category as larger "award-winning" nonprofits, all of which had more capital than I did. I was mostly proud of the fact that one of my launching tenets still remained: even with a small budget, we could have a big impact. The rewards were evidence of that fact.

With my confidence in our nonprofit soaring, I felt ready for the next step in C2A's journey: expanding to another city. Atlanta is such a large city, and a new nonprofit seemed to be opening every day. I felt as if the area were becoming saturated with nonprofits (which was not necessarily a bad thing), but such saturation resulted in everyone going after the same pool of money. I wanted C2A to keep helping people in Atlanta, which meant I'd have to expand or risk losing what we'd worked so hard to achieve.

On a rare vacation, my wife and I traveled to St. Simons Island, a small coastal town near Brunswick, Georgia, about four and a half hours southeast of Atlanta. Brunswick's history dated back to the Civil War, with historic homes dotting its landscape. But, by the time we'd vacationed there, the town had been experiencing historic poverty levels. I wondered, *What happened? How did it change?*

I learned that most of the jobs in the community were governmental, educational, or shipping-related, like unloading cargo ships. I also learned that the people in Brunswick seemed to have a special bond with each other, as if their collective poverty were a strong glue.

I relate all this because, right before this memorable vacation, I'd been debating myself about whether Birmingham or Savannah was supposed to be Contribute2America's next city to help. Both cities could have used our help, but I had no contacts in either place. Then Nicol and I went to Brunswick and everything became clear.

Denise, a friend of mine, had told me that her cousin, Sharon, worked for a nonprofit in Brunswick. Safe Harbor provided homeless children ages two to seventeen with a secure place to live. A couple of weeks after our vacation, I met Sharon at Safe Harbor and plied her with questions about what they did and what they needed. As if God had orchestrated this meeting long ago—which I fully believe he did—Sharon told me that their chief need was *meat*. Even though they received food from a few food banks, they seldom received enough meat. I immediately agreed to help.

The next month, as promised, I brought a freezer to Safe Harbor stocked with several hundred pounds of ground beef, chicken, and pork so that their children could have some proper protein. Since then, C2A has been supplying Safe Harbor with meat.

Joining up with Safe Harbor also helped me secure discounts from area food distributors who knew where their food would ultimately wind up. Maybe I shouldn't be surprised anymore, but I am still surprised when a for-profit business donates or discounts their goods for our nonprofit. I'm always thankful for their generosity, and I always try to let them know just how much their giving truly helps people in need.

One reason I was particularly glad to connect with Safe Harbor is that they minister directly to kids who have been abandoned by their parents. During my time as a patrol officer, I saw far too many such kids. Sure, their parents might have lived with them, but you could tell that the parents had checked out and that it was up to the kids to take care of themselves. I felt bad for them, but places like Safe Harbor gave me hope.

As C2A's work with Safe Harbor continued, Safe

Harbor ran into a problem: they had more children in need than they could house. After discussing what could be done, Sharon, Jeff, and I began a new program at Safe Harbor called Street Beat.

For the children who couldn't be admitted to the Safe Harbor house, they lived on the streets or with friends and relatives. We knew that many of them didn't have a chance of living that way for long. They'd eventually wind up in Child Services—or worse. That's why we designed Street Beat: to assist these kinds of kids with the basic necessities to help them make it through a week.

A local hospital donated a house where these children could come and be safe. They could wash their clothes or take a shower. We'd also supply them with a nightly meal or a small bag of snacks for the weekend, when the Street Beat house was closed. During the school year, the kids could come after school to complete their homework. We'd supply tutors to help them as well.

As Street Beat continued on and flourished, we discovered that many teens were aging out of Child Services but still needed help. In 2015, Safe Harbor started taking young adults between the ages of eighteen and twenty-three. Most of them were employed and/or attended college—life goals that, I imagine, many of them never expected to be able to attain simply because of their life circumstances. I am so grateful to have played a small role in that change.

As I learned more about the city, I found out that Brunswick also had a homeless problem. I reached out to the local Salvation Army, introduced myself and Contribute2America, and asked if we could start assisting them with their weekly feeding program. They readily agreed.

In less than a year, Brunswick had become Contribute2America's second location. I couldn't believe we were routinely helping so many people, both through our own efforts and our communal work with other nonprofits.

But one thought sometimes still wakes me up at night.

What more can we do?

CHAPTER 30

A CLOSING CHALLENGE

THROUGH ALL OF MY CHALLENGES, I never lost my joy for life.

"Joy is an emotion that's acquired by the anticipation, acquisition, or even the expectation of something great or wonderful."[1] So, if your passion is to serve others, I know you will find this joy again. There is no greater calling to serve others. When you do, that joy I am talking about will overcome you. It's so powerful you will want to do it again and again.

We all strive in our lives to do more, but, before you can succeed, you must be thankful for what you do have—and don't always look at what you don't have.

Life is hard, and we will all fail at some point. Some people need your help to get back on track, just as I needed help from others. My life has had many challenges, but I know that if we want to change the world, it starts with us.

The guest speaker at the 11Alive Awards was a rabbi. During his speech, he said something along the lines of, "We all want God to come down and fix our problem, but God is already here, and he works through each one of us to solve these problems of the world, like homelessness, childhood cancer, poverty, global warming, and racism. It's our duty to make this happen."

I want you to take some time away from your computer, your games, or your phone and walk outside. Look at what is going on in the world. You don't have to start a nonprofit to make a difference, but you may need to do more than what you're doing now. This can happen in many ways: help your elderly neighbor, volunteer, donate food, write a check, or call old friends who might be struggling.

Or start a community police program. Seriously. If your department does not have one, *you* need to start one. These programs will bring back what many departments have lost, and that is serving others. Community police programs help reduce crime and bring goodwill and partnership to the community. I have seen how these programs have transformed communities and the people who live there.

Whatever you do, do *something* worthwhile for the betterment of others. Just try it. I promise: that miracle you're looking for will happen and God will bless you.

My dream in life is that, when I leave this place, I'll know deep down inside that I've left it a better place than when I started.

I hope you'll do the same.

Together, let's keep asking: What more can I do?

---

1. Jack Wellman, "What Is The Biblical Definition of Joy? How Does The Bible Define Joy?", Patheos, May 21, 2015, https://www.patheos.com/blogs/christiancrier/2015/05/21/what-is-the-biblical-definition-of-joy-how-does-the-bible-define-joy/.

EPILOGUE: MY FRIEND JOE PT. II

REMEMBER JOE, my homeless friend who'd been living under a bridge in Atlanta for fifteen years prior to when I met him?

Remember Joe, who became my de facto liaison between me as an officer and his homeless neighbors?

Remember Joe, who gladly welcomed our Contribute2America assistance and made sure all the homeless communities he knew would know about us?

For as long as I knew Joe, I'd tried to help him escape homelessness. No person should have to endure that kind of hard existence for long, let alone for more than a decade. But Joe refused that level of help. His reason?

"I don't wanna be a burden to anyone."

After five years of trying, I didn't bring it up quite so often. Joe seemed set in his ways. Plus, I had to admit that I liked having Joe as my "in" with the homeless people he knew.

And it's not as if he didn't agree with me that remaining homeless was probably a bad idea. He wanted to clean up the bridges and get rid of the "bad homeless" just as much as I did. The "bad homeless" were the ones who'd engage in violence, drugs, or committing other crimes. Joe told me about certain members in his camp who'd break into cars and sell drugs.

Well, Joe's "snitching" got back to those "bad homeless" he'd been talking about.

One night, while sleeping on his tattered mattress under the bridge, Joe bolted awake in searing pain.

He was *on fire*.

The bad homeless had torched his bed while he was sleeping in it. By the severity of the act, I have to assume they wanted him dead.

But God didn't.

Joe was admitted to an area hospital for several weeks. With burns over 60 percent of his body, he'd required multiple skin grafts. After he was released from the hospital, he returned home—underneath the bridge. Since he didn't have proper care and lived in such squalid conditions, it wasn't surprising when his wounds became infected. Joe was admitted back to the hospital.

When he was released from his second hospital stay, I rented a hotel room for him for a month. I helped nurse him back to health. I got him into and out of the shower. I scrubbed and cleaned his wounds. I applied burn ointment, and I re-bandaged his wounds with clean bandages twice a day. I fed him three meals a day. Due to his alcoholism, I also did my best to help him through his withdrawal symptoms. I did this for almost a month until Joe got well.

During that time, he began rethinking his staunch position on his own homelessness. Even he couldn't deny that his "home" was no longer safe. He knew it was time to make a change he had long dreaded. When he was healthy enough to do so, Joe entered a program at the Atlanta Union Mission.

Today, Joe is a preacher at that facility. He mentors other homeless men and women. He may have suffered greatly to get to where he is, but Joe is living his calling to free people from the sometimes invisible bonds of homelessness. Because he was once like them, he's quite an effective witness—especially when he shows them the scars he still bears from the night his life forever changed.

I am immensely proud of Joe.

I am proud of Contribute2America.

And I hope I've made and will continue to make my brother John and my father, Robert, proud of me.

ABOUT THE AUTHOR

JEREMY TURNER is the executive director of Contribute2America.

In 2002, Jeremy joined the Dekalb County Police Department in Atlanta to help protect and defend his community. He had a vested interest in this mission, having lost his brother Jonathan to a hit-and-run drunk driver in 1998 and his father four months later to an armed robbery.

Jeremy worked as a uniformed officer until 2005 when he was promoted to detective with the Major Felony Unit investigating robbery/homicide cases. In 2008, he was chosen to spearhead an interactive, community-based policing program in his district/division.

Patrolling the streets of Atlanta, Jeremy quickly realized how isolated the city's homeless population really was. Many of the disenfranchised Jeremy encountered were veterans and families grappling with a myriad of issues, i.e., lost employment, a lack of affordable housing, domestic violence, mental illness, and chemical dependency.

This phenomenon struck a resonating chord with

Jeremy, whose brother Jonathan had served as a Marine in the Gulf War. He could also identify with struggling families because he has the responsibility for a wife and three children of his own.

Since then, Jeremy had dreamed of launching a program that would bring medical services, food, and supplies directly to the homeless. In addition, he wanted the program to serve as a liaison to expeditiously link those most in need to resources in the community.

His dream was fully realized in 2008 with the creation of Contribute2America (C2A), a nonprofit organization he founded to help fill the void in current services for Atlanta's homeless population. Jeremy won the prestigious 11Alive Community Award in 2012 for his work in Atlanta and the CEO Award for Dekalb County in 2013.

During the past ten years, Jeremy has served more than 500,000 pounds of food and assisted more than 100,000 people. He has carried his idea to Brunswick Georgia where he has expanded his mission.

Jeremy left the Dekalb County Police Department at the end of 2015 and currently works as a police officer with the Glynn County Police Department in Brunswick, Georgia.

Jeremy has expanded his model and is now working with other nonprofits assisting children who are currently in transition between foster care and DFAC.

Jeremy hopes to continue C2A's vision and mission in more cities throughout the country.

To learn more, visit Contribute2America.org.

To contact Jeremy Turner, email jeremy.turner@contribute2america.org or call 404-406-4088.

PART 7

APPENDIX: FIRST15 DEVOTIONALS

SEEKING TRANSFORMATION

The following seven devotionals are republished with permission from First15.org.

I have been encouraged and challenged by the devotionals provided by the ministry of First15, and it's my hope that this sampling will cause you to subscribe to their daily devotional, listen to their daily podcast, or visit their website at First15.org.

WEEKLY OVERVIEW

We serve a God of powerful transformations. All throughout Scripture God takes those whom the world deemed the lowest, the hopeless, and the helpless and uses them to change the world. You are not beyond transformation. God longs to break off that which inhibits you from experiencing fullness of life. He longs to heal you, deliver you, and set you free. May your life be forever changed as we spend time discovering God's heart for transformation.

"Create in me a clean heart, O God, and renew a right spirit within me." Psalm 51:10

WORSHIP

Song: "When You Walk Into the Room" by Bryan and Katie Torwalt

DEVOTIONAL

As humans burdened and suffering from both our sins and the fallen nature of the world around us, we are in desperate need of transformation. We are in desperate need of help from a God who has the power to not just clean us up on the outside but to transform us at the core of who we are. But this God doesn't force transformation on us. He works when we make space for him to do so. If we're going to experience the freedom, joy, and purpose that can only come from the inner working of the Holy Spirit, we must be those who seek transformation.

Psalm 51:10-12 says, *"Create in me a clean heart, O God, and renew a right spirit within me. Cast me not away from your presence, and take not your Holy Spirit from me. Restore to me the joy of your salvation, and uphold me with a willing spirit."* Here in Psalm 51 David exemplifies the heart of one who seeks transformation. He models for us a posture of humility that will lead to powerful encounters with God's transformative love. He doesn't sit back and merely live with that which plagues him but goes to God with his problems that he might be changed.

David begins as we all should in asking for God to do a

mighty work in his heart. And in this act of asking God to create in him a clean heart, David opens himself up to receive the powerful work of the Holy Spirit. To receive transformation from God we have to come before him humbly and honestly that he might have space to do the impossible in our lives.

Often we spend a majority of our efforts trying to convince others and ourselves that we don't need help. We work tirelessly to build up a facade that we have it all together. We do everything we can to maintain a sense of control in our lives—even in regard to our spirituality. But in doing so we place appearances above reality. We allow that which is destroying us from the inside to persist simply because we are unwilling to acknowledge that we have need. It's as if we tried to cover up an external wound with jewelry expecting the surface level beauty of something to contain the power to heal what's underneath. We don't need that which covers up. We need the healing that comes from going with an honest, open heart to the one true Healer.

God's heart for you and me today is that we would put down our guards, take an honest look at our hearts, and recognize our need for transformation. He longs for us to take a moment and call out that which is robbing us of the abundant life he so willingly died to give us. Your God is willing and able to transform you. That which has plagued you for so long will be healed and broken off your life if you will continually seek transformation from your loving heavenly Father. May you experience powerful transformation today as you enter into a time of guided prayer.

1. **Meditate on the importance of seeking transformation.** Allow Psalm 51:10-12 to be your model.

"Create in me a clean heart, O God, and renew a right spirit within me. Cast me not away from your presence, and take not your Holy Spirit from me. Restore to me the joy of your salvation, and uphold me with a willing spirit." Psalm 51:10-12

2. **Take an honest look at your heart.** Where do you need transformation? What lie, habitual sin, perspective, or fear is robbing you of abundant life? What's chaining you to the ways, cares, and burdens of the world?

3. **Declare your need for transformation in that area to God.** Tell him you need his help. Ask him to come and do a mighty work in your heart. Listen to whatever he would speak over you, and trust that he will transform you if you continually seek his help.

"If we confess our sins, he is faithful and just to forgive us our sins and to cleanse us from all unrighteousness." 1 John 1:9

We all have areas in which we need transformation. We all are in need of God's help. Not one of us is perfect. Rather than spending all your energy trying to keep up appearances with others, yourself, and with God, devote yourself completely to living honestly and humbly. Stop exhausting yourself doing that which is of no value and seek help. If you will commit to seeking continual transformation, your efforts will produce life and peace rather than more burden. May your heart be filled with hope as the Holy Spirit works in your life today.

Extended Reading: Psalm 51

GOD TRANSFORMS US INTO NEW CREATIONS

SCRIPTURE

"Therefore, if anyone is in Christ, he is a new creation. The old has passed away; behold, the new has come." 2 Corinthians 5:17

WORSHIP

Song: "How Can It Be" by Lauren Daigle

DEVOTIONAL

One of the greatest lies told to those who have been redeemed by the blood of Jesus relates to our old and new natures. So many believers live under the oppression of the lie that God in his grace may see us as clean, but at our core we're truly not. We live as if redemption in Jesus is like clean clothes covering up the dirt and filth that will always remain, and as if redemption is our get-to-heaven-free card. We hold fast to a belief that salvation was more of an illusion of redemption than an actual transformation. And those lies act like weights dragging us back to the ways and sins of our former selves.

Scripture could not speak more clearly of the opposite. 2 Corinthians 5:17-21 says:

Therefore, if anyone is in Christ, he is a new creation. The old has passed away; behold, the new has come. All this is from God, who through Christ reconciled us to himself and gave us the ministry of reconciliation; that is, in Christ God was reconciling the world to himself, not counting their trespasses against them, and entrusting to us the message of reconciliation. Therefore, we are ambassadors for Christ, God making his appeal through us. We implore you on behalf of Christ, be reconciled to God. For our sake he made him to be sin who knew no sin, so that in him we might become the righteousness of God.

If you are in Christ today—if you are saved—then you are a new creation. The old hasn't stuck around until you die; *"The old has passed away; behold, the new has come."* You see, the fact that you have been transformed into a new creation doesn't have anything to do with your sins, failures, and beliefs. Transformation in Jesus is based on his power, not yours. Truth is based on his sacrifice, not your actions. You are a new creation totally and completely by the grace of God, apart from any of your works—as righteous or sinful as they may be. *"For our sake he made him to be sin who knew no sin, so that in him we might become the righteousness of God."*

Don't live today with your experience as your truth. Don't see yourself based on your works but rather on the truth of what Scripture says about you. If you will begin to believe that God truly has already transformed you into a new creation and reconciled you to himself simply by grace, then you will live and act on a foundation that births freedom and righteousness. But, if you set your mind on the things of the flesh, which is in opposition to the reality of transformation already worked in you at the cross, then you will live chained to the ways of your former self (Romans 8:6).

Take time today to reflect on your new nature in Jesus. Allow Scripture and the Holy Spirit to help you see yourself as one transformed and set free by grace. Commit yourself to live with grace as your source rather than your own strength. And experience freedom today that comes from living with a renewed mind.

GUIDED PRAYER

1. **Meditate on your new nature in Christ.** Allow Scripture to be your foundation for truth, not your experience.

"Therefore, if anyone is in Christ, he is a new creation. The old has passed away; behold, the new has come." 2 Corinthians 5:17

2. **Where does your life not line up with the truth that you are a new creation?** What is entangling you to the things of the world? Where are you not experiencing the life of the Spirit?

"For God has done what the law, weakened by the flesh, could not do. By sending his own Son in the likeness of sinful flesh and for sin, he condemned sin in the flesh, in order that the righteous requirement of the law might be fulfilled in us, who walk not according to the flesh but according to the Spirit." Romans 8:3-4

3. **Confess any sin to God and ask for his**

help in living by the Spirit. Ask the Spirit for a revelation of what it looks like to live with him as your source rather than your own strength. Ask him for a heart-level revelation of your new nature.

"I have been crucified with Christ. It is no longer I who live, but Christ who lives in me. And the life I now live in the flesh I live by faith in the Son of God, who loved me and gave himself for me." Galatians 2:20

Foundational to living a life that lines up with truth of who God says you are is living by grace. In our own strength we can accomplish nothing. We have no power over sin in and of ourselves. We have no power to live free from the ways of the world when we try to live based on our works. That's why Romans 8:3 says, *"For God has done what the law, weakened by the flesh, could not do."* He fulfilled the requirement of the law that we might live by grace. He set us free from living in our own strength by filling us with the Holy Spirit, our great Helper. Stop living in your own strength and learn to live by grace. Learn to feel, think, and act on the foundation of grace. Your heavenly Father who loves you has given you all you need to live as a new creation. He has done it all. So take hold of who you are in Jesus and experience a life transformed by the reality of God's power and love.

Extended Reading: Romans 8

CONTINUAL TRANSFORMATION

SCRIPTURE

"I appeal to you therefore, brothers, by the mercies of God, to present your bodies as a living sacrifice, holy and acceptable to God, which is your spiritual worship." Romans 12:1

WORSHIP

Song: "In The Morning" by Chris & Jessie Miller

DEVOTIONAL

Oftentimes we see transformation as a one-time act. We find a problem and work on it until it gets better, then we go back to living life as normal. But the heart of God is for continual transformation. God longs that we would be so open and aware of the desire of the Spirit that we allow him to transform us every moment of every day.

Too often we just accept that we are who we are as if

the God we serve didn't have the power to continually set us free. We live as if the Holy Spirit is a God who only shows up every now and then to shake things up then retreats back into the heavens. But God is both loving and present. He is always there for us. He is always filled with desire for us. And the Holy Spirit is constantly ready to lead us, in love, out of the darkness and into the marvelous light of abundant life.

So what does continual transformation look like? How do we live in sync with the Spirit who can constantly change us from the inside out? Romans 12:1 says, *"I appeal to you therefore, brothers, by the mercies of God, to present your bodies as a living sacrifice, holy and acceptable to God, which is your spiritual worship."* Continual transformation will come when we decide to stop living for ourselves and instead become a living sacrifice to God as our *"holy, acceptable"* act of *"spiritual worship."*

You see, when we live for ourselves we naturally take control of our own lives and therefore subjugate God and his desire to transform us. When our limited perspective on what's good in life guides us rather than the perfect, transcendent perspective of God, we will only receive transformation from God when we desperately need it. But, when we seek to be a living sacrifice to God at all times our hearts become open to all the Spirit is doing, saying, and feeling in every moment. If you want to be continually transformed by the powerful, life-changing love of God, you have to choose every day to center your life around the will and desires of God.

Psalm 139:23-24 says, *"Search me, O God, and know my heart! Try me and know my thoughts! And see if there be any grievous way in me, and lead me in the way everlast-*

ing!" May David's prayer be our prayer today as we enter into a time of guided prayer.

GUIDED PRAYER

1. **Meditate on God's heart to continually transform you.** Reflect on his nearness and his desire to heal you, deliver you, and empower you.

"The Lord your God is in your midst, a mighty one who will save." Zephaniah 3:17

"Fear not, for I am with you; be not dismayed, for I am your God; I will strengthen you, I will help you, I will uphold you with my righteous right hand." Isaiah 41:10

2. **Take a moment to assess your heart.** Are you seeking to be a living sacrifice to God in all you do? Or are you living with your own desires and will as the foundation of your life?

3. **Decide to be a living sacrifice today.** Decide to live with the desires and will of God as your foundation. Center your life around the goodness, nearness, and power of your loving Father.

"I appeal to you therefore, brothers, by the mercies of God, to present your bodies as a living sacrifice, holy and acceptable to God, which is your spiritual worship." Romans 12:1

Choosing to be a living sacrifice is a daily decision. Without spending consistent time in God's presence there is no hope for continual transformation. It's only when we encounter the kindness of God that we are able to respond with surrender. It's only upon meeting with God that we live with his power and love as our foundation. Living sacrificially is not something you do in your own strength.

Rather, it is the natural response of those who see God for who he truly is. May you commit yourself to experience the reality of God's presence today. And may your life be an act of worship in response to the great love you've been shown.

Extended Reading: Psalm 139

TRANSFORMATION THROUGH EXPERIENCE

SCRIPTURE

"And we all, with unveiled face, beholding the glory of the Lord, are being transformed into the same image from one degree of glory to another. For this comes from the Lord who is the Spirit." 2 Corinthians 3:18

WORSHIP

Song: "Forever (Live)" by Kari Jobe & Bethel Music

DEVOTIONAL

No Christian practice can take the place of experiencing God. It's in experiencing God that we begin to live in response to the unconditional, unfathomable depths of God's love. It's in experiencing God that we learn to discern and trust his perfect, pleasing will. And it's in experiencing God that our hearts are transformed into powerful reflections of his wonderful character.

2 Corinthians 3:18 says, *"And we all, with unveiled face, beholding the glory of the Lord, are being transformed into the same image from one degree of glory to another. For this comes from the Lord who is the Spirit."* When we see God face-to-face everything changes. You can't see God and stay the same. Encountering him always requires something from us. Experiencing his holiness always calls us to be holy as he is holy (1 Peter 1:15). Experiencing his love always calls to love because he has *"first loved us"* (1 John 4:19). And experiencing his heart for transformation always calls us to surrender our lives to him as a *"living sacrifice, holy and pleasing"* (Romans 12:1).

In Isaiah 6:1-6, Isaiah's encounter with the living God speaks to the truth of transformation through experience. In response to seeing *"the Lord sitting upon a throne, high and lifted up"* and hearing the Seraphim calling to one another, *"Holy, holy, holy is the Lord of hosts; the whole earth is full of his glory,"* Isaiah's natural response was, *"Woe is me! For I am lost; for I am a man of unclean lips, and I dwell in the midst of a people of unclean lips; for my eyes have seen the King, the Lord of hosts!"* And upon declaring the truth of his depravity a seraphim touches his lips with a burning coal and says, *"Behold, this has touched your lips; your guilt is taken away, and your sin atoned for."* Isaiah was transformed through experiencing God.

If you want your life to be transformed you must set out to seek the face of God. You must respond daily to his invitation to meet together. Your life must be centered around the fact that perfect, blameless Jesus gave his life that you might simply have relationship with the Father. If you do— if you give your life to experience the fullness of God's love, power, and presence—you will never be the same. May you "[behold] the glory of the Lord" today as you enter into a time of guided prayer (2 Corinthians 3:18).

1. **Meditate on the transformation that takes place in experiencing God.**

"And we all, with unveiled face, beholding the glory of the Lord, are being transformed into the same image from one degree of glory to another. For this comes from the Lord who is the Spirit." 2 Corinthians 3:18

"Behold, this has touched your lips; your guilt is taken away, and your sin atoned for." Isaiah 6:7

2. **Turn your heart to God and seek his face.** Have faith that when you set aside time to experience God he will manifest his presence to you. His presence is his promise.

"You have said, 'Seek my face.' My heart says to you, 'Your face, Lord, do I seek.'" Psalm 27:8

"You will seek me and find me, when you seek me with all your heart." Jeremiah 29:13

3. **Rest in the presence of your loving Father.** Confess any sin you have in response to his holiness and promise to forgive you. And receive the cleansing that comes from repentance.

"Repent, then, and turn to God, so that your sins may be wiped out, that times of refreshing may come from the Lord." Acts 3:19 (NIV)

"If we confess our sins, he is faithful and just to forgive us our sins and to cleanse us from all unrighteousness." 1 John 1:9

So great is God's love for you that he longs to meet with

you. In Revelation 3:20 God says, *"Behold, I stand at the door and knock. If anyone hears my voice and opens the door, I will come in to him and eat with him, and he with me."* God is already knocking on the door of your heart. You don't have to wonder if he will meet with you when you open your heart to him. Revelation 3:20 is his promise. He longs for you to encounter him more than you do. He wants to be known by you more than you want to know him. Have faith in the goodness of your God and live a lifestyle of encounter. May your life be transformed by a revelation of God's unfailing love and presence.

Extended Reading: Revelation 3

GOD MEETS US IN OUR WEAKNESS

SCRIPTURE

"My grace is sufficient for you, for my power is made perfect in weakness." 2 Corinthians 12:9

WORSHIP

Song: "Saviour King" by Hillsong Chapel

DEVOTIONAL

The ways of God are radically different than what we experience in the world. The world tells us that only the strong survive. The world values those who can take care of themselves. We're taught to look to our own strength as our source. We're taught never to let others see our weakness. But God values those who acknowledge their weakness in humility. His heart is for the destitute, the needy, and the lost. Jesus spent his valuable, limited time with the prostitutes, tax collectors, lepers, and sinners. And as a result, we who can never be perfect, who even at our best still can't cut it, have renewed hope.

In 2 Corinthians 12:9 Paul writes, *"But he said to me, 'My grace is sufficient for you, for my power is made perfect in weakness.' Therefore I will boast all the more gladly of my weaknesses, so that the power of Christ may rest upon me."* True growth and transformation aren't the result of working in our own strength. We can't change ourselves no matter how hard we try. Transformation is only possible when we declare the truth of our weakness, stop living in our own strength, and receive the power of a loving, present God. Transformation comes when we make room for the Holy Spirit to fill us, empower us, and set us free, not because we are deserving of his help, but because he loves us.

Psalm 103:14 says, *"For he knows our frame; he remembers that we are dust."* God doesn't expect perfection from us. He knows perfection is unattainable. And instead of perfection he asks for honesty. Instead of valuing our strength he values our humility. What he asks of us, all of us can give. All of us can boast of our weaknesses as Paul did. All of us can look at our lives and declare our need for God's grace. And in doing so we receive power from on high. In acknowledging that *"we are dust"* we gain the help of an Almighty, all-loving, ever-present God.

Stop trying to attain perfection in this life. Stop finding your value and identity in what you do. And look to God as your strength. Allow his love, power, and help to be your source. Live in light of the truth that his strength is both able and available to you. May you enter into a season of peace founded on the limitless grace and power of your heavenly Father.

1. **Meditate on God's heart to meet you in your weakness.**

"But he said to me, 'My grace is sufficient for you, for my power is made perfect in weakness.' Therefore I will boast all the more gladly of my weaknesses, so that the power of Christ may rest upon me." 2 Corinthians 12:9

2. **In what ways are you living in your own strength?** Where do you need to stop striving and receive the grace and help of God?

"For he knows our frame; he remembers that we are dust." Psalm 103:14

3. **Declare your weakness to God and receive the power of his presence.** Ask him how he wants to help you. Make space in your heart for the Holy Spirit to strengthen you and empower you.

Proverbs 22:4 says, *"The reward for humility and fear of the Lord is riches and honor and life."* God has riches, honor, and life in store for you as you live in his strength. He longs to lead you to fullness of life if you will be willing to enthrone him as Lord over your heart. May you be founded on the grace and help of God and experience fullness of life today in the presence of your loving Father.

Extended Reading: Psalm 103

RESURRECTION CULTURE PART 1

Scripture: *"I am the resurrection and the life. Whoever believes in me, though he die, yet shall he live."* John 11:25

Song: "Spirit Break Out" by Jesus Culture

Through the resurrection of Jesus, we have been given the opportunity to live life in a new way. Romans 6:4 says, *"We were buried therefore with him by baptism into death, in order that, just as Christ was raised from the dead by the glory of the Father, we too might walk in newness of life."* The power of the resurrection is not just over our deaths, but over our lives. God didn't just pay for our freedom for all of eternity, but for right now—for this very moment. He's calling you and me to live a resurrected lifestyle. He's ushering us into a resurrection culture.

Romans 8:9 says, *"You, however, are not in the flesh but in the Spirit, if in fact the Spirit of God dwells in you. Anyone who does not have the Spirit of Christ does not belong to him."* 2 Corinthians 5:16-17 even says, *"From now on, therefore, we regard no one according to the flesh. Even though we once regarded Christ according to the flesh, we regard him thus no longer. Therefore, if anyone is in Christ, he is a new creation. The old has passed away; behold, the new has come."* Your life is changed because of Jesus' death and resurrection. Because Christ rose from the dead, you have been raised from spiritual death.

Too often we are content to live our lives apart from the present reality of new life in Jesus. Too often we are satisfied living according to the flesh when we have been given a whole new way of living according the very Spirit of God who dwells within us as believers. Romans 8:1-2 says, *"There is therefore now no condemnation for those who are in Christ Jesus. For the law of the Spirit of life has set you free in Christ Jesus from the law of sin and death."* We have been freed from condemnation through the new law of the Spirit ratified by the death and resurrection of Christ. *"There is therefore now **no** condemnation."* Let that sink in for a minute. Through the grace of God, not by anything you could ever do, you have been freed from condemnation. The only one who could ever truly condemn you is now your heavenly Father. You are the child of the only Judge, and he has offered you continual and uncompromising pardon because of his love for you.

And past being pardoned from condemnation, Romans 8 tells us that we have now been crowned as co-heirs with

Christ. Romans 8:16-17 says, *"The Spirit himself bears witness with our spirit that we are children of God, and if children, then heirs—heirs of God and fellow heirs with Christ."* Because of the life we have been given in the Spirit, we are *"fellow heirs with Christ."* I'm not sure we even fully understand all that means for us. So often we live as if we are forced into submission to the world. We live according to the principles of the flesh rather than life in the Spirit. You have been freed from slavery to sin. You have been freed from the condemnation of the world. Christ defeated the enemy at the cross, and through him you have obtained total and complete victory. You are now crowned with Christ and given his authority to see heaven come to earth through your life.

And most importantly, Romans 8 concludes by telling us of the incredible love available to us in our resurrection and victory with Christ. Romans 8:37-39 says, *"No, in all these things we are more than conquerors through him who loved us. For I am sure that neither death nor life, nor angels nor rulers, nor things present nor things to come, nor powers, nor height nor depth, nor anything else in all creation, will be able to separate us from the love of God in Christ Jesus our Lord."* There is nothing you or anyone else could do to separate you from the love of God. Through Christ's resurrection, you have been offered unchanging and unshakable love. Living life in the Spirit is living with the constant knowledge that you are and will forever be loved.

Spend time today allowing the word and presence of God to stir up your desire to live according to the Spirit rather than the flesh. We'll look tomorrow at how we can practically live this new life available to us, but for today simply allow God to reveal his unceasing love for you.

1. **Meditate on the life available to you in the Spirit.** Allow your desire to walk in fullness of life to be stirred up by God's word.

"There is therefore now no condemnation for those who are in Christ Jesus. For the law of the Spirit of life has set you free in Christ Jesus from the law of sin and death." Romans 8:1-2

"The Spirit himself bears witness with our spirit that we are children of God, and if children, then heirs—heirs of God and fellow heirs with Christ." Romans 8:16-17

"No, in all these things we are more than conquerors through him who loved us. For I am sure that neither death nor life, nor angels nor rulers, nor things present nor things to come, nor powers, nor height nor depth, nor anything else in all creation, will be able to separate us from the love of God in Christ Jesus our Lord." Romans 8:37-39

2. **Reflect on your own life.** Where are you still living your life according to the flesh? Where do you feel condemned or unloved? Where do you feel conquered rather than a conqueror?

3. **Ask the Lord to guide you into life in the Spirit today.** Life your live with a renewed mind according to God's word.

As you go throughout your day, know that you have the choice to live your life differently. You are not bound by the way you've lived your life in the past. There is *"newness of life"* available to you every single day through the power of the Spirit working in you as a believer. Yield to the Spirit's leadership and live in light of the freedom purchased for you by the death of Jesus.

Extended Reading: Romans 8

RESURRECTION CULTURE PART 2

SCRIPTURE

"We were buried therefore with him by baptism into death, in order that, just as Christ was raised from the dead by the glory of the Father, we too might walk in newness of life." Romans 6:4

WORSHIP

Song: "Holy Spirit (Live)" by Kari Jobe (Live) ft. Cody Carnes

DEVOTIONAL

We devoted time yesterday to searching Scripture for understanding on life in the Spirit. We looked at Romans 6:4 which says, *"We were buried therefore with him by baptism into death, in order that, just as Christ was raised from the dead by the glory of the Father, we too might walk in newness of life."* And in Romans 8 we learned that God has offered us a life free from condemnation (Romans 8:1-2), crowned us with Christ as his co-heir (Romans 8:16-17) and made it so nothing could separate us from the depths of his love (Romans 8:37-39).

We've been given an incredible life in the Spirit through Christ. But so often we continue to live as if his death and resurrection didn't change our everyday occurrences. So often we live according to the flesh rather than our new life in the Spirit. So, building on the foundation of God's word, let's take time today to learn some practical ways we can better live the abundant life afforded to us through the resurrection of our Savior.

How can we better live our lives in the Spirit? How can we experience the *"newness of life"* Paul talks about in Romans 6? It all starts with growing in our friendship with the Spirit. The Bible tells us that the Spirit prays for us when we don't know what to pray (Romans 8:26), that he teaches us (John 14:26), helps us (John 14:16), and fills us (Ephesians 5:18). But the Holy Spirit never forces himself on us. He only fills and speaks when he is asked. Such is the depth of God's love for us that he waits patiently for us to open ourselves to him, beckoning us with his loving-kindness. So, we must make time every day to be filled with the Spirit anew and learn what it is to receive his help, teaching, presence, and prayer. It's only when we grow in our relationship with him in private that we will learn how to be led and used by him in public. Just as you couldn't pick out an unfamiliar voice from a crowd, you will have a hard time feeling the nudges of the Holy Spirit in this rushed and busy world without experiencing him in the secret place. Growing in friendship with the Spirit is vital and foundational to living with *"newness of life."*

Next, we have to live in obedience to God's word. God

has blessed us with an incredibly practical book meant to guide us into an abundant, Spirit-filled life. To walk in obedience to the word is to live a life experiencing all that God has in store for you. So, spend time in the word of God opening your heart to the Spirit. Allow him to be your teacher. And commit yourself to live in obedience to what he shows you. In obedience to God's word you will discover how perfectly applicable and powerful Scripture is to your life.

Lastly, set aside time to simply receive the love of God. We live our lives in a society full of people and possessions that promise to satisfy us. We're surrounded by a world that isn't living out of personal experience with God and isn't a reflection of his truth. If we're going to live in the world but not be of it, as Romans 12:2 commands us, we must spend time experiencing the reality of God's love. We must allow his presence to be the lens through which we see the world around us. Victory over the enemy comes from encountering the reality of God's unfathomable grace and affection. Following the leadership of the Spirit moment to moment stems from encountering the reality of his nearness in the secret place. You have to spend time engaging in spiritual relationship to live a spiritual life.

Spend time today growing in your friendship with the Spirit, reading God's word, and receiving the love of your heavenly Father as you enter into guided prayer.

GUIDED PRAYER

1. **Spend time receiving a fresh filling of the Spirit.** Simply open your heart and wait for him. Ask him to make the reality of his presence known to you. Ask him to lead you into deeper friendship with him. The Spirit loves

to talk to us, help us, and guide us because he loves us. You will never have a better friend than the Holy Spirit.

"Or do you not know that your body is a temple of the Holy Spirit within you, whom you have from God? You are not your own." 1 Corinthians 6:19

"But the Helper, the Holy Spirit, whom the Father will send in my name, he will teach you all things and bring to your remembrance all that I have said to you." John 14:26

"If you then, who are evil, know how to give good gifts to your children, how much more will the heavenly Father give the Holy Spirit to those who ask him!" Luke 11:13

2. **Spend time engaging with God's word.** Where does your heart need more life? Where do you feel like the world has taken over? Look up Scripture on whatever subject you need help with, and stand on God's word! Renew your mind and live in obedience today.

"All Scripture is breathed out by God and profitable for teaching, for reproof, for correction, and for training in righteousness, that the man of God may be complete, equipped for every good work." 2 Timothy 3:16-17

3. **Receive the love that God has for you today.** Similar to receiving a filling of the Holy Spirit, just spend time resting in the presence of God. Ask him to reveal his love to you. Ask him how he feels about you.

"I am the vine; you are the branches. Whoever abides in me and I in him, he it is that bears much fruit, for apart from me you can do nothing." John 15:5

"As the Father has loved me, so have I loved you. Abide in my love." John 15:9

I pray that you would be transformed as you align your life with the resurrection culture. May you see yourself as one saved, redeemed, empowered, and delivered. May you live in pursuit of the abundant life available to you. May the chains of this world fall off in light of God's powerful grace. And may your life be a reflection of the reality of Jesus' life, death, and resurrection.

Extended Reading: John 15

ACKNOWLEDGMENTS

I would like to thank my lovely wife, Nicol, and my children: Hannah, Mary, and Jamilee. They have put up with me and continue to help me with this adventure.

Especially Nicol—you have always encouraged me and helped with every fundraiser, provide medical attention to the needy, and cook food for several hundred people with no complaints. I love you more for this support than words can ever express.

Tad, thank you for jumping in and assisting when I had no one to help in the beginning. You are a true friend and a great firefighter, and because of you this dream became a reality.

Thank you, Mom, for raising me with compassion and empathy for others. You have instilled in me what it means to help others through your many years of nursing. You have carried and supported me through all of the good and bad times. I could not have asked for a better mother.

To my wonderful sister. Your heart is as big as mine and you never turn a cheek to go out of your way and help others. Because of you and your children, the Thanksgiving feeding program would not have worked. Thank you for your dedication to this cause.

To all of my other family members, you have provided support and guidance. Thank you!

I would like to thank all of my brothers and sisters in law enforcement. All of you put your lives on the line to help others and serve the public just as I have. You are the true meaning of *heroes*.

I would like to thank Angel Armor, who provided me with a protective bulletproof vest and for the company's model of protecting law enforcement.

I would like to thank all of my family and close friends, like Joe, Shane, Chad, and Chris, for being there for me during the worst time of my life. Without your support, I am not sure I would have made it through that hardship.

Thank you, Brian, and all of the others who assisted me in setting up the nonprofit. I appreciate all of your kindness and believing in this cause. None of this could have been possible without you donating your time and business experience to form Contribute2America.

I would like to thank Craig Denison from First15. Because of your words and inspiration, you guided me to complete this project that has been going on for four years in the making. If you are out there struggling, please get the First15 app or visit First15.org. Its words will open your heart to other possibilities. If you just want to start your day with worship, get the app.

To my editor, Blake Atwood, without you, this dream of writing a book would have not become a reality. You took my mess and turned it into something worthy. You believed in this book when no one else did. I will be forever grateful for your support, patience, and guidance.

To my teammate, Tom, you supported and believed that

my story needed to be told. Thank you for your words of encouragement on how this story could pursue greatness in others, reach other public safety agencies, and spread the importance of community involvement.

To my brother, John, and Dad. I miss you both every day. I think how our lives would be different if you guys were still here. I wish you could have met Nicol and our children. I know they would have loved you guys. When I look at my children, I see each of you in them, from their smiles and qualities you passed down from our family genetics. I hope you are looking down on me and keeping me safe on the job and are proud of what I am doing.

I have met several thousand homeless men and women over the years, but Joe is my family. I could not have done it without you as you could not have accomplished what you did without me. We make a great team.

I would like to say thank you to all the staff at C2A and the volunteers who keep the wheels running. Because of you, we have been able to continue serving others for almost ten years.

Last but not least, I would like to say thank you, God.

God has blessed me, strengthened, me and encouraged me throughout my life. God has always had a hand in my life due to the foundation my grandmother provided. I hope and pray that he will walk with you as he has with me.

Thank you to all of the financial supporters who believe in me and our mission. Without you, we could not do it.

— Jeremy

53202915R00112

Made in the USA
Columbia, SC
11 March 2019